How to do SELF LOVE

Break through unworthiness, master self-confidence and be happy every single day.

Diana Mikas

Praise for Diana's work

Now I know that I am worth so much more than sitting back and trying to co-dependently do everything and waking up 10 years from now repeating the same cycle. I am so happy I met you, Diana.

—Amy Dooner

I was attracting individuals that would put me in a position of not knowing who I was, getting lost, always agreeable and not speaking up. I lost myself. I was depleting my internal happiness and I became empty... The magic happened when I looked at the trauma of my inheritance... it's mystical, it's magical what happened. It's a game-changer as to how you view yourself. My relationship with my mother has now blossomed when the healing happened. I'm no longer empty. I'm full of love. I feel pumped, secure... the integrity in me is beyond.

I will never ignore my red flags again. I was a zero when I started working with Diana and now I'm a 9.5 in my happiness factor!

—Nikki DeGagne

I was in a place where I wasn't sure of myself and wasn't sure if I did the right thing breaking up. It's for anyone, honestly, even if you're in a good relationship. Because I feel the value, whether you're in a happy relationship or not, is that you really start to dig deep into how you were brought up, the relationships you've been around and what you consider healthy and what you are telling yourself. You don't get to do this work, even in therapy. I feel like it's such a good investment in yourself, that can only strengthen all relationships, whether you're in a relationship or not. It's totally worth it.

—Bridget McCrory

I was the fixer and I've realized through this that I can't be. It's not my responsibility and it's not my job. I loved every second of this. It came at the perfect time of my life.

I had to go through this, I would have just kept going through the cycle of who I was and this was my opportunity to finally grow. I always tiptoed around hard conversations and felt guilty. Being able to communicate my feelings was really big for me. Boundaries and communication were big learning for me! And figuring out my love inheritance made everything change. I love how you had me rethink things and how I ask for things now. I'm so happy and thankful that I took a chance on myself.

I feel like a new woman!

—Deanna Ziouras

Please note the information contained within this document is for educational and entertainment purposes only. All effort has been executed to present accurate, up to date, and reliable, complete information. No warranties of any kind are declared or implied. Names have been changed to protect the privacy individual clients.

Readers acknowledge that the author is not engaging in the rendering of legal, financial, medical or professional advice. The content within this book has been derived from various sources. Please consult a licensed professional before attempting any techniques outlined in this book. By reading this document, the reader agrees that under no circumstances is the author responsible for any losses, direct or indirect, which are incurred as a result of the use of the information contained within this document, including, but not limited to, — errors, omissions, or inaccuracies.

Catalogued in Library and Archives Canada

Hardcover ISBN: 978-1-7388752-2-1

Paperback ISBN: 978-1-7388752-1-4

E-book ISBN: 978-1-7388752-0-7

TABLE OF CONTENTS

STEP #3
Create Your Happy Life
(Self-Confidence)

BEGINNING NOTE

A study published in the *Journal of Clinical Psychology* [1] found that women tend to have lower self-esteem than men. The *National Institute of Mental Health* [2] reports women are twice as likely as men to experience depression. The statistics don't lie. Women don't regard themselves as highly as they should.

They find it hard to connect with who they are on the inside - what they stand for and what to believe in. Many women are unable to recognize their authentic selves. So, it is difficult to come to terms with their uniqueness, mistakes, and parts that are hard to face in the mirror. Self-confidence among women is not what it should be, and rightly so, when we often feel pressured to play a certain role or fit a certain stereotype. The hard truth is that most women are living unhappily and unfulfilled. They lack self-love.

Can you relate to these facts? Are you struggling with feelings of worthlessness, negative thoughts and self-perception, and a lack of confidence in your abilities? Do you find it challenging to make decisions that prioritize your well-being and instead focus on the needs of others? Are setting boundaries and protecting your time and energy difficult, or are you fearful of displeasing others? Do you find it hard to trust and have difficulty attracting and maintaining loving relationships with partners, family, and friends?

If you answered yes to even one of these questions, I applaud your bravery in owning your truth. And I want you to realize you are not alone. Many women struggle with self-love at some point in their lives. It is, after all, a personally uncharted journey. But the good news is that you can break through feelings of unworthiness and cultivate self-love and self-confidence along this journey.

Imagine learning to love yourself wholeheartedly and unconditionally, as you are today, rather than striving for an idealized version of yourself that commercialized society says you should be. If you developed self-confidence and a strong sense of self-worth, you would walk with your head held high and feel personal power and dignity. With that would come the ability to make decisions that align with your values and goals and a resistance to being swayed by the opinions of others.

A strong sense of self-worth also leads to greater self-acceptance, including being comfortable with your appearance and any perceived imperfections or flaws. Your uniqueness is your ultimate strength. By focusing on positive thoughts, gratitude, and self-care, you nourish and replenish your physical, mental, and spiritual self. And you'll cultivate a sense of self-empowerment and well-being that would otherwise never happen.

Confidence and knowing you belong right where you are don't have to be unattainable goals. They must not. They will become your reality once you commit to a journey where you'll make three essential stops:

1. Self-awareness
2. Self-acceptance
3. Self-confidence

The signs will be evident as they lead you to the final stop on this journey: self-actualization through self-love. Contrary to what you have been told, self-love is not buying another pair of shoes or indulging in alcohol or sugary treats but rather the unwavering commitment to your mental, physical, and spiritual well-being.

Self-love is characterized by giving yourself space and compassion, feeling reassured about your worth, investing in your growth and development, and engaging in self-encouraging behaviors. Love of self manifests in practical ways such as walking through life with ease and confidence, feeling secure in your being and personal goals, and attracting like-minded individuals who are also working towards self-love. You will find it easier to navigate challenges and setbacks and to pursue your passions and ambitions with determination and resilience.

No one else can journey to this place for you. You need to be the one who commits to taking each step, even those that are difficult to navigate. Taking this trip is your responsibility. You owe it to yourself for one simple reason. You deserve the best this life has to offer; nothing trumps love that shines from the inside out.

This path is only yours to travel, but it does not have to be a lonely walk. Let this book be your companion. Let it be the guide that makes this trek, not one filled with strife and turmoil but rather one gratified with wondrous discovery.

Think of these pages as a map. Step by step, you will:

- Learn to recognize the factors (including your love inheritance, the role models you had growing up, and your lived experiences) that affect your ability to love yourself.

- Explore how ancestral trauma creates emotional layers known as "Heart Armour" that blocks the love you want from getting in.
- Discover how your present-day emotional intelligence becomes the filter through which you receive and send love.
- Easily identify and challenge negative thought patterns that may be holding you back.
- Embrace self-care practices that nourish and replenish your physical, emotional, and mental well-being.
- Develop the base to build self-confidence and self-acceptance through small steps with self-compassion.
- Cultivate gratitude and shift your perspective to focus on what your heart truly desires.
- Master how to connect with others and build supportive relationships that help you feel loved and valued.

After years of heartache, your Heart Armour can become thick and impenetrable, leading to loneliness, isolation, anxiety, panic, and fear of the future. Attracting loving partners, family, and friends can seem like a never-ending puzzle you can't solve. But there is hope.

Whether struggling with unworthiness or looking to improve your self-confidence, this book will take you on an unexpected journey. I will share with you the 3-step process that thousands have used to help them break through their love blocks and start loving themselves and others. To find that unconditional love within, we must dismantle the stories hindering your progression. We will deconstruct the patterns that aren't working only to rebuild the ones that will lead you to your authentic self - the self you lost along the way.

We'll explore the importance of self-love for overall happiness and fulfillment and how it can benefit you and those around you. Additionally, this book will address common misconceptions about self-love and help you understand why prioritizing your well-being is not selfish or egotistical. With the help of client stories, you will see that you are not alone in this quest.

This is Your Journey

Finding self-love is a journey. As with any other existential journey, there will be challenges, setbacks, and opportunities for growth and healing. It is normal to encounter difficulties and make mistakes along the way. You may also receive negative feedback or criticism from others during your shift. It is important to remember this is a transformational process, and it is normal to have doubts or struggles. Be kind and gentle with yourself. Take what you need and be inspired by the possibility of another way.

I hope you turn back to these pages when you encounter the inevitable. Come back to these words to regain your center and focus. Come back to remember why you started the journey and why it is essential that you continue.

Through these pages, I fulfill my mission to help women rediscover self-love and the love of their lives. My holistic approach combines energy and scientific practices, nutrition, and life coaching to provide a multifaceted methodology for healing and transformation. We have to address all of the areas for complete healing. I will highlight the effectiveness of the strategies taught in this book with client stories and the progress they have seen using them.

I've dedicated the past decade to this mission because I know what it is like to believe that you are doing everything right, only to have that illusion of happiness crumble around you. My divorce from a 20-year marriage shattered everything I held as the truth about myself. As I struggled to dig my way out of the pit of despair, I realized the false image we've all been sold - that we should be compliant, compromising, and self-sacrificing - is no longer sustainable.

Ultimately, we are relearning that we have undeniable and infinite power. The true, ultimate strength of that power can only be found by loving ourselves fiercely and unconditionally.

I hope this book serves as a valuable resource and guide for anyone seeking to love themselves more fully and who wants to live happier and more fulfilled lives. With the right tools and mindset, you can reclaim your true self with the deepest love and create the life you desire.

So, if you're ready to embark on *your* journey, I invite you to take the first step by going to www.howtodoselflove.com/resources where you'll find the tools you need to accompany your journey toward self-love.

STEP #1

Clear Your Foundation (Self-Awareness)

Your task is not to seek for love,
but merely to seek and find
all the barriers within yourself
that you have built against it.
Rumi

CHAPTER 1

Find the Cracks

Self-love is recognizing and accepting your worth and value as a human being. It involves a sense of self-respect and self-acceptance, solidified by a commitment to caring for and nourishing your well-being. Self-love does not encourage the ego self or foster self-aggrandizement. It is also not about holding yourself in higher regard than others. Instead, it is about being conscious that your needs and well-being are just as important as the needs of others and taking steps to prioritize and care for yourself.

Self-love is essential to a healthy and fulfilling life because it is the root of developing a healthy and loving relationship with yourself. However, the journey toward self-love does not begin with actively seeking it. Self-love is not something that can be found. Instead, it is an ongoing process of evolution where patience and compassion are needed. You must also develop a willingness to learn and grow. This journey is unique to each individual and is greatly rewarding.

The first step taken on this journey is to identify and dismantle the barriers you have built within and around yourself. These barriers manifest in many forms, like self-doubt and negative self-perception. They also unfold in unhealthy behavior patterns like overeating, being unable to say no when you are overwhelmed, or simply not wanting to take up a task.

This chapter guides you through the process of identifying these barriers - the cracks on the road to self-love - so you can finally heal them and let them go. By examining your current behaviors, thought patterns, and external circumstances, you can better understand the obstacles blocking you from self-love. Once these barriers are identified, you can work on dismantling them to build a strong foundation of self-worth and self-acceptance. This process is essential for beginning your journey toward living a fulfilling and meaningful life.

Anatomy of Heartbreak

The most common circumstance comes in the form of a relationship gone wrong. Because it's through our relationships that we are challenged to see the parts of us that need dismantling and rebuilding. Once we see where we are on this first stop of the journey, we can chart a new path back to ourselves. But first, let's review what statistics say about heartbreak and divorce as an indication of where we are.

Heartbreak comes early in life. First breakups happen in the same age range. At least 35% of teens between the ages of 13 and 17 have been in a romantic relationship, according to *Pew Research Center* [3].

The median age at which women tend to marry in the US is 28 years as of the year 2022, says the *United States Census Bureau* [4], while the divorce statistics highlight 30 years old as the average age couples tend to divorce. Nearly half of all marriages in the US conclude in divorce or separation. About 60% of all divorces include people between the ages of 25 and 39 years [5]. The *United States Census Bureau* [6] reports that this figure sharply increases upward at 40 years old. They conclude, "While 34% of women and 33% of men ages 20 or older who ever married had ever divorced, the percentage of adults 55 to 64 years divorced is much higher."

Breakups are not just limited to romantic affiliations. Breakups are a natural part of social interactions and can be an inevitable and sometimes necessary part of relationships. From the time we are young, we form close relationships with peers similar to us in age, gender, and interests. These friendships are an essential source of social support and emotional well-being.

As we grow and develop, our friendships expand to include a broader range of personalities, including individuals of different ages and demographics. Just as romantic relationships end, so do friendships at times. We can even have falling outs in family relationships. Breakups can occur for various reasons, including changes in circumstances, feelings, or priorities or a failure to communicate effectively or resolve conflicts.

The common thread is that breakups break our hearts. Those feelings are compounded as we grow older, and the instances of heartbreaks we experience accumulate. Based on the statistics highlighted above, we are unlikely to get out of our teens without experiencing it in some form or the other.

When we are in healthy and supportive relationships, they provide us with a sense of belonging, validation, and self-worth. These types of relationships can foster a sense of self-love and help us to feel more confident and secure in ourselves. On the other hand, heartbreak can be a difficult and painful experience that takes a toll on our emotional and physical well-being. It can be incredibly challenging when feelings of rejection, abandonment, or betrayal accompany the heartbreak. Feeling hurt, angry, and vulnerable in these situations is natural. It is also common to experience a sense of loss and grief as we try to adjust to the new reality of our lives.

Unfortunately, heartbreak can also make it more challenging to love ourselves. You may feel less worthy or deserving of love, or you may blame yourself for the failure of the relationship. You may struggle with negative thoughts and self-perception or engage in unhealthy behaviors to cope with your pain. You may also find that you are attracting the same types of partners that have caused you pain or feel unsure about navigating the dating scene after a long absence.

If you feel stuck and unable to move on from the pain of your breakup, it is a sign that it is time to address the heartbreak and heal from the past. When you carry the weight of heartbreak, it blocks you from experiencing the love you desire. You may have found temporary comfort in your pets and family, but you yearn for a loving, supportive, and fulfilling relationship. You can create a brighter and more fulfilling future by releasing the pain and rebuilding your self-worth and self-love.

To move forward, you must first discover where you are in your pain. By acknowledging the various effects that can occur when the heart is broken, we must come to terms with the anatomy of heartbreak and the 6 phases associated with it. See Figure 1.

Figure 1. Anatomy of Heartbreak

Shock

Heartbreak can leave you feeling staggered, especially if it is unexpected. It digs up a well overflowing with various emotions, including sadness, anger, and disappointment. The events that led to the heartbreak can feel as if they are not real or happening to someone else. During this time, it is normal to experience physical symptoms, such as difficulty sleeping and changes in appetite. You may also feel as if you are constantly running on empty.

Trauma

Heartbreak is a traumatizing experience, and so after shock comes a familiar realization unlocked in your memory. The stress response is a natural and necessary mechanism that helps us cope with challenges and threats. It perpetuates through activating a series of physiological and behavioral responses designed to help us respond and adapt to the stressor. A complete system alarm goes off.

This extreme stress leads to the formation of energetic heart armor. It is natural to want to protect yourself from pain and heartbreak, and building a wall around your heart can be a way to try to do this. However, building a wall can also prevent you from experiencing the full range of emotions and connections that are a part of life. It can create a barrier to intimacy and prevent you from forming deep, meaningful relationships with others.

Pain

Pain and anger are intertwined. Sometimes the pain comes first, and sometimes anger.

Your body may feel grief as pain. Your breath stops. Your stomach may be in knots. The physical response may be so intense that your heart reacts with what is known as Takotsubo Myocardiopathy – a heart attack. More common is the deposit of pain in a particular area that relates to a part of your body that aligns with an imbalance of a Chakra. We will explore this later.

Anger

Anger is the next phase characterized by fury at yourself, someone else, or the situation. Anger impacts your ability to think straight or think critically. It can also lessen self-control and lead to self-sabotaging behaviors like eating and drinking for comfort.

Although we've been taught to suppress our anger, this emotion is not inherently "bad." No emotion is. All feelings should be honored and felt to their full extent so we can move past them. The important thing is to find healthy ways to express your anger. Remember that it is okay when you make mistakes during this time. Give yourself grace and take the time you need to heal.

Denial

Denial is a common coping mechanism. It involves refusing to accept the reality of the situation or not being able to acknowledge the magnitude of the loss. Therefore, you might bargain to try to keep the connection you had or rationalize trying to hold on to it with "*if only I had*" thinking.

During this stage, feeling numb, disconnected, or disbelieving is common. You may try to distract yourself from the pain or avoid thinking about the loss altogether. But these emotions demand to be processed so you can move on, no matter how difficult.

Isolation

Isolating yourself after experiencing heartbreak is a natural response. You may feel like you're protecting yourself from further emotional pain as it serves as a way to cope with intense emotions. However, isolation tends to have negative

consequences, often leading to feelings of loneliness and disconnection. A lack of desire to have social interactions is a common sign of this phase, but so is the resistance to doing things you previously loved to do.

As you identify which stage you are at, remember that everyone experiences heartbreak differently. It's okay if you're in more than one phase of the process. The pain can be terrible but try to recognize that heartbreak is an opportunity for growth and self-reflection. This opportunity allows you to heal and move on with time and support.

Be patient. Physical health plays a massive role in the healing process, as it only happens when the body is ready to accept the recovery. As uncomfortable as it is, take your time with this process. We live in a world that is becoming increasingly anxious and fearful. Many people lead stressful lives that place them in chronic anxiety and hyper-alertness. If you are in this state, remember this is exactly where you need to be.

To begin the healing process, explore the underlying causes of your unhappiness, whether it be a divorce, the loss of a loved one, or generational trauma. By identifying these cracks and working through them, you can begin reconciling the past to create a more positive outlook on life.

Reconnect to Yourself

The previous section was meant to help you develop an awareness of what's happening with your body during heartbreak. Now let's set the stage for healing with grounding.

Loving yourself places you in a unique position to be fully connected in the present moment and to your physical body. Your mind is not focused on the past or worrying about the future. Instead, your emotions and senses are more fully immersed in what is happening right now, which brings more profound joy and fulfillment in even the simplest things.

When you're not fully connected in the present moment and your physical body, a feeling of overall disconnection from your emotions, physical sensations, and surroundings forms. This feeling of disconnect describes the state of being ungrounded, which causes anxiety and stress as you are likely also to feel disconnected from your abilities and resources to handle challenges. It becomes difficult to be present in your relationships and activities. It is also hard to be fully engaged in tasks and hobbies.

Being ungrounded affects your energy connection and chakra system. Energy connection is the energy flow between beings or objects. There is an energy flow between you and other people and everything in the environment. This energy can occur on a physical, emotional, or spiritual level.

You will be filled with vitality, happiness, and a sense of well-being when your energy is balanced and flowing freely. There is also a flow of energy within you as your physical body interacts with your spiritual, mental, and emotional energies. This flow affects your overall well-being and quality of life. On the other hand, if you have an unhealthy energy connection within yourself, the disconnect from your own body and emotions leads to a range of negative physical and emotional symptoms.

There are energy centers in your body called chakras. They are metaphysical "spinning disks" that act like portals to your endocrine system. When we experience heartbreak, depression, or anxiety, we look to the chakras to help us find balance again.

For example, if your root chakra (located at the base of your spine) is blocked or unbalanced, you will experience anxiety and detachment from your body. You may struggle with feelings of love and connection and experience difficulty with relationships if your heart chakra (located in the center of your chest) is blocked or unbalanced. A blocked or unbalanced throat chakra (located in the throat area) leads to difficulty expressing yourself and communicating effectively. These are just a few examples, but imbalances in any chakra can manifest in various ways and affect your overall well-being.

Ungroundedness occurs because your energy is not fully connected to your physical body and the present moment, as you discovered in the Anatomy of Heartbreak (Figure 1). Being ungrounded hinders your ability to process and move through difficult emotions, such as those that arise during a heartbreak. You will first work on grounding yourself and strengthening your connection to Mother Earth and your physical body to navigate better and heal from challenging experiences.

Let's begin with the root chakra to ground yourself more securely in the present moment and your body.

Ground Your Root Chakra

The root chakra or first chakra (also known as the Muladhara in Sanskrit) is associated with grounding, stability, nourishment, the ability to trust, and a sense of belonging. It is represented by the color red and is the foundation of your energy system. Its primary function is to keep you connected to the physical world and in your body. A balanced and free-flowing root chakra makes you feel grounded, secure and connected to your life. See Figure 2.

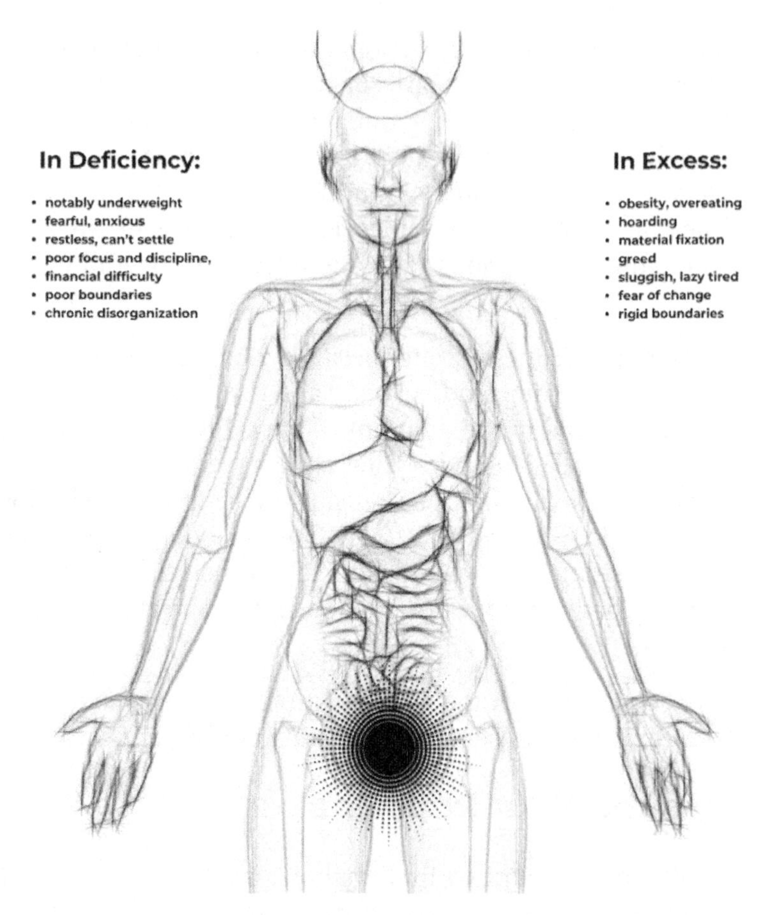

Figure 2. Root Chakra

Traumatizing events like birth trauma, abandonment, physical neglect, poor physical bonding with one's mother, major illness or surgery, and physical abuse create discord in the energy flow of this chakra. A deficiency in the root chakra manifests in various ways, both physically and emotionally.

Some of the common symptoms of deficiency include:

- Being underweight or malnourished
- Feeling fearful, anxious, and restless
- Having difficulty in settling or poor focus and discipline
- Having weak boundaries
- Chronic disorganization
- Suffering from financial difficulty

Excess energy flow in the root chakra leads to the following:

- Overeating and obesity
- Hoarding
- Fixation on material things
- Overspending

When this chakra is out of balance, feelings of insecurity, fear, and disconnection from your body and the physical world arise. Physical symptoms also manifest and can include:

- Lower back pain
- Problems with the legs and feet
- Issues with the immune system
- Problems with the colon or rectum

During times of heartbreak, the root chakra can become unbalanced. The associated intense emotions and stress can cause the root chakra to become overactive so that feelings of anxiety and insecurity develop. It can also become underactive, leading to feelings of disconnection and detachment from the physical world. [7]

To bring a sense of grounding and stability during heartbreak, ensuring the balance of the root chakra is a must. The result will be a calming of the nervous system. When the nervous system is in a state of balance, the body and mind function optimally. When out of balance, the body and mind may experience stress, anxiety, fatigue, and other harmful effects. You can calm down the nervous system with techniques or practices that help relax and regulate it.

Luckily, plenty of ways to calm the nervous system include fascial release, meditation, yoga, deep breathing, touch therapy such as hugs and massage, yoga, and physical activity to get you back into your body. Such practices help activate the body's natural relaxation response and bring the nervous system back into balance.

In addition, engaging in activities that bring you joy, practicing self-care, nourishing the physical body with healthy foods, and getting sufficient rest can also help calm the nervous system's energy. Connecting with the earth through activities such as gardening or hiking can also be beneficial. Working with a healer or therapist specializing in energy also promotes a sense of grounding and connection to the physical body.

For quick relief, you can begin with these simple techniques.

Practice the Mantra LAM

A mantra is a word or phrase repeated frequently, often as a form of meditation. The repetition helps to overcome negative thoughts or emotions, increasing mental clarity, and focus and promoting healing and well-being.

I like to do this one in the shower first thing in the morning, but you can also do it before you get out of bed. With deep belly breathing, say the mantra, "LAM," ten times as you visualize the grounding core at the base of your spine flowing down to the center of the earth.

Affirmations

Affirmations are positive statements or declarations used to challenge and overcome negative thoughts or self-sabotaging beliefs. They affect the levels of consciousness by replacing negative thoughts with positive ones. The use of affirmations can rewire our beliefs and influence our reality, and change the way we think, the way we feel, behave, and experience life. Also known as the law of attraction, it suggests that we attract into our lives whatever we focus on, whether positive or negative.

"The earth supports me and meets my needs."

"I easily release that which I no longer need."

"I am truly loved and supported always."

Say these words with conviction and believe in them as you say them. Also, write them down and place them somewhere visible as a reminder to focus on their meaning throughout the day. Repeat these affirmations to yourself daily or whenever you feel anxious or nervous.

Re-establish Your Integrity

Be aware of when you deny the reality of the situation or blame yourself for the fallout. Or when you pretend that everything is okay when it is not. These are all forms of lying to yourself, and they may be practices that you do (consciously or unconsciously) to cope with the pain and discomfort of heartbreak. While they provide temporary comfort, they ultimately undermine your integrity and prevent true healing and growth.

Lack of integrity leads to unhappiness, as noted by Martha Beck in her book *The Way of Integrity*.[8] This lack of integrity can manifest in the form of lying, both to others and to ourselves. These lies can be used to connect our fantasies of who we wish we were.

"Integrity is the cure for unhappiness. Period," says Martha, revealing how to move beyond this sabotaging pattern. Integrity is about being honest and authentic to oneself. It's about aligning your actions and words with your values and beliefs. But what does integrity truly entail? It can be challenging to practice if you have not been exposed to examples of integrity.

Society and leaders often don't demonstrate integrity through their actions, typically failing to follow through on promises. Similarly, our parents may not have modeled integrity for us through their behavior. It becomes more challenging to understand what it means to be honest and trustworthy to yourself and to act following your values and beliefs. It can also make it harder to trust others and recognize when we lie to ourselves under the guise of the other person lying.

Developing integrity means taking a long, hard, deep look into yourself to start being honest and transparent with yourself and others. Make it a practice of paying attention to your thoughts and behaviors. Listen and observe as objectively as possible and ask yourself if your thoughts and actions align with what you believe to be true. You will notice moments when you engage in self-sabotage or self-betrayal. It also encourages accountability for your actions, taking responsibility for your mistakes, and trying to do what is right, even when it may be difficult or inconvenient. Awareness precedes taking steps to address negative thoughts and behaviors.

Another approach to re-establishing your integrity is to practice honesty and vulnerability with others. Sharing your thoughts and feelings with trusted friends or a therapist helps you stay on track to make positive changes in your life. They can give you alternative points of view about your thoughts and actions as well as help you confront and challenge negative beliefs you hold about yourself.

Stronger, more nurturing, and loving relationships can be formed when you open yourself up to others. Being vulnerable gives the people in your life permission to also be vulnerable. To develop this further, you must be reliable and stick to your word. Be mindful of doing so within the parameters of your boundaries. Additionally, engaging in activities that promote self-reflection and self-care builds a stronger foundation for self-love and self-acceptance.

Meredith's Story

Meredith's journey with her second husband highlights the damaging effects of lacking integrity in a relationship and with oneself. She gathered the courage to separate from him, but he begged her to let him back into her life, claiming to have changed. She got roped back in, and they resumed their relationship.

Soon after, he was diagnosed with leukemia. Meredith is a nurturing soul, and her caretaking nature kicked in. She quickly fell back into the role of doting partner again, even though her intuition questioned whether he planned it this way, knowing he was sick. Despite her doubts, she supported him through doctor visits and admission into the cancer clinic.

Meredith soon discovered that he was lying again. Plus, he had started a GoFundMe campaign to pay for his leukemia treatment, but instead of using the money as intended, he bought a hot tub and a purebred dog.

Finally, the deception was revealed when a woman showed up while Meredith and her husband were having coffee one day. The stranger announced that she had been coming over during the day for sex and making pornography with him while Meredith was at work. Even though she was heartbroken, Meredith felt guilty and couldn't leave him.

Meredith's story is a powerful example of how heartbreak can shatter our sense of self-worth and self-love. Despite feeling strong and independent before her relationship with her now ex-husband, she was immobilized by guilt and low self-worth. This is a common experience for women in toxic or abusive relationships, as manipulation and gaslighting cause them to doubt their perceptions and feelings.

She believed all the complementary language from this man and the putdowns. He would tell her that she was a trophy wife, only to turn around and tell her that no one else would want to date her. He was a master at planting seeds of doubt in her head. His ploys were successful mainly because she never felt good enough as a child. She craved praise and attention from him - things she never got from her parents. She let him back into her life three times. But if she had heeded the red flags, she never would have gone down that path again.

It's understandable to feel vulnerable after experiencing heartbreak. You may also be more susceptible to being drawn back into unhealthy relationships like Meredith. Prevent such handicaps by seeking support to rebuild your self-worth and self-love. Support is the key to creating healthy, fulfilling relationships in the future.

Meredith did just that when she came to me for help and guidance. We worked on her foundational cracks and reconnected her root chakra so that she could set healthy boundaries and protect herself moving forward as she healed.

When you change your energy and become more grounded, those around you may rebel or fall away. It is the natural process of finding yourself again, as witnessed when

Meredith's husband stalked her after she left the final time. He tried to guilt her into taking him back again with narcissistic gaslighting statements like, "All I ever wanted to do was love you. I can't believe you're doing this." But by this time, Meredith had the support she required and quickly got a restraining order so he could not legally come onto her property again. She also blocked him from all forms of communication. She did what she could not do before – establish firm boundaries that were true to her goals and values. No matter your circumstances, you can also re-establish your integrity in the same way.

Begin with a Promise to Yourself

To reclaim your integrity, become aware of the cracks in your foundation and take steps to address them. Establish awareness of where you are now at the beginning of your journey. Create a calm nervous system by addressing any imbalances in your root chakra. Remember, stress and anxiety hinder your ability to make decisions that elevate and uplift you. An unbalanced root chakra prevents creating mindful intentions that keep you grounded in the present.

Revisiting past traumas, developing a stronger sense of self-worth, setting healthy boundaries, and learning to be honest with yourself and others are part of the journey. By focusing on your well-being and inner truth, you can live a more fulfilling and authentic life based on a solid foundation of self-awareness.

Join me to learn these grounding techniques here www.howtodoselflove.com/resources

CHAPTER 2

Discover Your Story

To understand how we got to where we are today, we must examine our previous experiences and how we have embraced them. This process of self-reflection helps us become more aware of the unconscious patterns and beliefs that have shaped our lives and influenced our actions. By educating ourselves about how the mind works and how we have lived many of our days in an unconscious state, we can identify and challenge negative thought patterns or behaviors that have been holding us back.

A critical aspect of this process is discovering your inherited love story. The story you are telling yourself is rooted in past experiences. It reveals the patterns and beliefs about love and relationships you have learned from your family and society. These beliefs take up a narrative like the pages of a novel and repeat in your thoughts tens of thousands of times daily.

I am not saying that this story is inherently wrong. This story can be negative or positive, but the likelihood of it being on the opposing end of the spectrum is higher as human beings have the propensity to think negatively.

Here are the facts about the thoughts going through your head right now. Science used to believe the average person has about 12,000 to 60,000 thoughts per day. According to a research study from Queens University in Canada[9], the new thoughts, which are part of a chain of thoughts, or thought worms, are estimated at 6200 thoughts per day. However, we still believe that 80% are negative and 95% are the same repetitive thoughts from the day before.

Negativity is hotwired into our DNA as a survival mechanism. It has created beliefs that are likely no longer serving you. This negative chronicle may be about yourself or your abilities or a fear of change or failure. These patterns are limiting and prevent you from finding true happiness and fulfillment.

To find your true happy self, you must be brave and examine and challenge your inherited love story to gain insight into how it has influenced your choices and relationships. Only then can you rewrite it to align with your authentic self and desires. Let's get started on doing just that.

Past Experiences Change the Brain

The mind is a mysterious entity comprised of many levels. Like a great explorer, you must examine it to understand how it works. On this journey, you will discover where to look for the stories that keep you stuck in unhappiness patterns.

According to the theories of Sigmund Freud, the mind is divided into three levels of consciousness: the conscious mind, the preconscious mind, and the unconscious mind. The conscious mind is what we are aware of at any given moment, while the preconscious mind consists of thoughts and memories that are not currently in our conscious awareness but are easily brought to the surface. The unconscious mind is composed of thoughts, memories, and desires outside our conscious awareness and is often difficult to access. When it comes to healing from past trauma, being aware of and in touch with all levels of consciousness helps us process and work through our experiences.

Carl Jung, a Swiss psychiatrist, psychoanalyst, and a close associate of Sigmund Freud, eventually developed his own unique theories about the human psyche. Jung's work was influential in the development of modern psychology and is still widely studied today.

One of Jung's most notable contributions to psychology is his theory of the collective unconscious, a universal, inherited part of the human psyche that contains archetypes or universal patterns or themes present in the myths, legends, and religious traditions of all cultures. According to Jung, the collective unconscious shapes our thoughts, feelings, and behaviors and can be accessed through dreams, myths, and other symbolic expressions.

Jung also developed the concept of individuation, which is the process of becoming a fully realized, integrated individual. He believed that this process involves integrating the conscious and unconscious parts of the psyche and bringing the opposing elements of the mind into balance.

Other key concepts in Jung's theory include the idea of the persona, which is the image we present to the world, and the shadow, which represents the unconscious aspects of our personality that we tend to repress or deny. Jung believed that we could achieve greater self-awareness and personal growth by becoming aware of and integrating these unconscious aspects of ourselves.

Like Jung's "shadow" side, past trauma can have a significant impact on our unconscious and conscious minds. Trauma can cause changes in the brain's structure and function and how the brain processes information and responds to stress. For example, trauma can disrupt the normal functioning of the amygdala, a region of the brain involved in processing emotional responses. This disruption can lead to an exaggerated stress response and an increased risk of developing conditions such as anxiety and post-traumatic stress disorder (PTSD). Trauma can also affect the prefrontal cortex, which is involved in decision-making, problem-solving, and regulating emotions.

On a deeper level, past trauma can also affect how we perceive and understand ourselves and the world around us. It can shape our beliefs, values, and ways of interacting with others, leading to patterns of thought and behavior that are influenced by the trauma.

At the highest level, past trauma can impact our sense of identity and how we see ourselves in the world. It can affect our sense of purpose, meaning, and fulfillment and may lead to feelings of disconnection, isolation, and a lack of belonging.

Thankfully, we've discovered that the brain is capable of neuroplasticity, which means it can change and adapt [10]. As such, it is possible to recover from the effects of trauma and to learn effective coping strategies to manage stress and emotions.

The Impact of Generational Trauma

Many women like you and I carry with them the influences and experiences of their parents, grandparents, and partners throughout their lives. These experiences can shape our perceptions, beliefs, and behaviors, including how we navigate relationships like romance and friendships. For example, if a person's parents had a tumultuous or unhealthy relationship, they are likely to carry these patterns into their relationships, even if they are unaware of it. Similarly, if a person's partner is unfaithful or abusive, it can impact their future relationships and trust in others. These past experiences will continue to exert influence over your current affairs and sense of self unless you become aware of them and then take steps to address and heal from their adverse effects.

Our love inheritance is the sum of these experiences. Some people have inherited positive, healthy patterns and backgrounds. Such a love inheritance allows these individuals to form secure attachments with others, feel confident in their self-worth and value, and be able to communicate and express their needs and boundaries in relationships. Part of this inheritance is also likely to involve a strong sense of empathy and understanding towards others and the ability to form and maintain healthy, supportive relationships with a sense of mutual respect and trust.

I mentioned an essential component of any relationship in the previous paragraph: secure attachment. It is one of four types of attachment styles. About 50% of the population attaches this way in relationships [11]. That leaves billions of other people who attach insecurely. Before we look at the ramifications of that, let's delve into what attachment styles are.

Discover Your Attachment Style

Attachment styles refer to how people behave in relationships (particularly in close and intimate relationships) and how they emotionally connect with others. Attachment styles are formed in early childhood, typically due to our experiences with primary caregivers, such as parents or other family members. There are four main styles: secure, anxious-preoccupied, dismissive-avoidant, and fearful-avoidant. Let's begin by exploring the secure attachment style.

A positive and secure connection with others characterizes a secure attachment style. People with this attachment style tend to feel comfortable with intimacy and can express their needs and emotions healthily. In childhood, there is an excellent likelihood of a strong, positive bond between this person and their primary caregiver, usually their parent or parents. The caregiver is emotionally available and attuned to the child's needs. This bond is characterized by the child feeling safe and secure and the caregiver responding consistently and sensitively to the child. Children with secure attachments feel comfortable exploring their environment and are more likely to be resilient and have better social skills.

The other three attachment styles are collectively grouped as insecure, but they hold different characteristics. Anxious-preoccupied attachment style is characterized by a strong desire for close relationships and a fear of being rejected or abandoned. This attachment style is often formed in individuals who have experienced inconsistent or unreliable caregiving during childhood, leading to a fear of abandonment and a lack of trust in others. People with this attachment style may have difficulty regulating their emotions and may struggle with confidence and insecurity in relationships.

These individuals may have experienced their caregivers as unreliable or unavailable, making them believe they cannot rely on others for emotional support. As a result, they may become overly dependent on others for emotional fulfillment and have difficulty regulating their emotions. They may also struggle with low self-esteem and a sense of inadequacy, leading to a constant need for validation and reassurance from others.

The dismissive-avoidant attachment style - is characterized by a strong desire for independence and a lack of desire for close relationships. People with this attachment style may have difficulty expressing emotions and avoid intimacy and commitment in relationships. This attachment tends to develop when a child lacks responsiveness to their needs growing up. As a result, the child learns to suppress their needs and emotions, thus forming a pattern of dismissing or avoiding close relationships to protect themselves from potential rejection or abandonment.

Fearful-avoidant attachment style is characterized by a mixed desire for close relationships and a fear of being rejected or abandoned. People with this attachment style tend to have difficulty trusting others and expressing their needs and emotions in relationships. A fearful-avoidant attachment style may develop in a child who has a caregiver who is abusive or neglectful. This behavior can make the child feel unsafe and unable to trust others, leading them to have ambivalent feelings about intimacy and closeness in their adult relationships.

How we give and receive love as an adult is affected by how we were given love in childhood. This factor is also indicative of how we love ourselves. We inherit much from our parents. And unfortunately, many of us have had generational trauma passed on to us as well, which has influenced the type of relationships we enter, how we behave in these relationships, and what we accept from others.

Generational trauma refers to the transmission of the effects of trauma from one generation to the next. Transmission can happen through various means, such as passing down coping mechanisms or behaviors that are unhealthy or self-destructive or through the direct communication of traumatic events or experiences. According to a study by Rachel Yehuda and Amy Lehrner on *Intergenerational transmission of trauma effects*, you have inherited the nervous system trauma response from your great-grandmother[12]. Think about that for a moment. How was your great-grandmother's life?

Generational trauma can significantly impact the mental and emotional well-being of individuals and communities. The outcomes tend to be negative, including difficulty with relationships, poor physical and mental health, and a lack of trust or connection with others – signs of a toxic love inheritance.

Holders of an unhealthy love inheritance tend to have past relationships that hold characteristics like the following:

Invalidation

Your feelings and experiences are not acknowledged or validated. You feel that your emotions are not important or legitimate.

Control

Your actions and decisions are controlled or manipulated by other people. You may feel like you have no autonomy or agency in your own life.

Gaslighting

Your partner may constantly deny reality or manipulate the truth to make you question your perception of events.

Emotional abuse

You are emotionally manipulated and intimidated.

Rejection

You are consistently rejected or abandoned by the other person. As a result, you may feel unworthy and unlovable.

Stonewalling

Your partner refuses to communicate or engage in any form of emotional or physical intimacy, causing you to feel isolated and disconnected.

Lack of trust

The other person consistently breaks promises and displays dishonest behavior, making you feel uncertain and anxious in the relationship.

Do you recognize any of these listed characteristics as part of the anatomy of your past relationships? Perhaps there were even elements of physical abuse where the other person used physical force or threats of physical harm to intimidate or control you.

After suffering such trauma, it can seem like there is no hope for change or the better. But I assure you that there is a rainbow beyond the clouds. You can heal from generational trauma and trauma inflicted by past relationships. You have taken the first step to overcome this and have created awareness that you have fallen into toxic thought patterns and behaviors that prevent you from having relationships that uplift and fulfill you. You can make the conscious choice about which patterns to keep and which to let go of so you can create healthy, fulfilling relationships.

We can change our genes to alter our reality. This process is called epigenetic modulation. It refers to how environmental factors affect gene expression without changing the underlying DNA sequence. It is a process through which the activity of specific genes can be turned on or off in response to environmental cues, such as diet, stress, and exposure to toxins. Epigenetic modulation can have short-term and long-term effects on an individual's health and behavior, and it is thought to play a role in developing many diseases and disorders.

Through epigenetic modulation, that is, by consciously developing a positive growth mindset, we can completely alter how our bodies function and accomplish many other feats that help improve our sense of self-worth, confidence, and happiness. We can also transform our emotional and mental health with deliberate, conscious effort. Let's discuss this in the next section.

Healing the Past

Thomas Hubl's book, *Healing Generational Trauma*, highlights that childhood trauma can have a lasting impact on an individual's mental health and relationships if it is not adequately addressed and resolved. In his words, "Trauma breaks relation. Within a person, trauma fractures relation to the self and sabotages connection to the other." [13]

Trauma causes disruptions in a person's sense of self and ability to connect with others. And it further perpetuates the cycle of trauma as it is passed down to the next generation and the next. However, it is possible to heal from trauma and break this cycle by facing the pain and learning how to cope in a healthy manner. After all, attachment styles are not necessarily set in stone and can change over time with the right interventions and experiences.

The aim is to get as close as possible to achieving secure attachment when forming relationships as you move forward.

It is not productive or helpful to blame your parents if you have discovered that you have displayed signs of an insecure attachment style. Attachment styles are formed based on a complex interplay of genetic, environmental, and experiential factors.

While parents do play a role in the development of attachment styles, it is crucial to recognize that they may not be fully aware of the impact of their actions and behaviors on their children. Also, please remember that everyone makes mistakes and that it is possible for parents to work to improve their parenting skills and create a more secure attachment with their children, no matter their age. It is more productive to focus on understanding and addressing the root causes of insecure attachment styles and working towards healing and building secure attachments in the present and future.

As mentioned earlier, you can change the love inheritance your parents, guardians, and past experiences passed onto you on a genetic level. There is even a specific formula for doing this, which looks like this:

Awareness + Forgiveness = Unconditional Love

Let's break down each part of the formula.

Awareness

Awareness involves becoming conscious of the patterns and behaviors passed down to you and how they may impact your current relationships. You must be open and honest about your past experiences and how they may shape your present.

Another aspect of awareness is being mindful of your thoughts and emotions. Pay attention to your inner dialogue and notice when you're having negative or self-defeating thoughts. Follow this up by challenging these thoughts. Reframe them in a more positive and supportive way.

Finally, you must be aware of your own needs. Set limits with others and be honest about what you're comfortable with and what you're not. You need to develop the ability to communicate your needs to your partner and loved ones. With this awareness comes the opportunity to make conscious choices about how you want to live and interact with others.

Forgiveness

Forgiveness is the process of actively working on letting go of anger, resentment, and other negative emotions towards someone who has harmed or wronged you, including yourself. You acknowledge and accept the harm that has been done but also choose to let go of the negative feelings and move forward with positive energy.

This process is challenging. However, it is also a compelling and liberating experience as it allows you to release the burden of negative emotions. We will dive deeper into working on forgiveness in the next chapter.

Unconditional Love

Unconditional love is a powerful force. It is the type of love that is given freely, without any conditions or expectations. It is a love that is based on acceptance and understanding rather than judgment or criticism. Combining awareness and passionate forgiveness can create a sense of unconditional love for yourself and others.

To cultivate unconditional love, you must learn to love and accept yourself just as you are without trying to change or fix anything about yourself. You also must forgive yourself for past mistakes and let go of any negative self-perceptions or self-doubt.

Unconditional love for yourself paves the way to developing a deep sense of compassion and understanding toward others. You learn to see others as human beings, with their unique struggles and challenges, rather than as perpetrators or obstacles. More importantly, you can let go of the victim story once you've mastered this formula.

By cultivating unconditional love for yourself and others, you can create a positive and transformative shift in your love inheritance story for generations in the past and the future.

Dismantle the Effects of Your Inherited Love Story

Healing from trauma can be a complex and emotional process. It involves facing memories and emotions we may have been avoiding or suppressing. But the journey to self-love passes through the valley where the pain and sadness of our past experiences reside. Ignoring or trying to avoid our pain will only cause it to fester and potentially erupt in unhealthy ways in what I call the Volcano Effect.

We often resist facing our past pain because we don't want to feel that pain again. However, if you're already feeling pain every day because of things left unsettled, it's worth confronting that pain to heal. You will never change it if you're afraid of reliving the pain. This fear keeps you in the loop of going through the same trauma time and time again. This loop is where you will remain stuck until you take a deep breath and bravely face the past.

One way to do this is to approach it with a mindset of exploration and understanding rather than with fear and avoidance. Viewing it as an opportunity to gain knowledge and awareness, you can find answers and change your love story. This process doesn't have to cause additional pain if you approach it this way.

Healing deep-seated trauma is crucial for finding confidence and a sense of worth because it allows you to understand and address the underlying causes of your unhappiness. It also allows you to find lasting solutions that improve your self-worth. Without this knowledge, you will continue to feel stuck and powerless to change your circumstances. By acknowledging and processing our pain, we can begin to heal and move towards a healthier, more fulfilling future. Keep in mind that your story is your own and that you can change the direction it takes at any time. Choose today to make that change.

Continuing Meredith's Story

Meredith's grandmother on her mother's side was a strong, God-fearing woman who pushed through a difficult life on a farm with 12 kids. She even cared for her husband as he died, even though he cheated on her and sexually abused their children. Despite all of this, Meredith looked up to her grandmother and wanted to emulate her strength and perseverance in her own life, as demonstrated by her own marriage.

Meredith's inherited love story was to keep strong and push through even with someone who was a philanderer and child abuser.

No doubt, Meredith's grandfather was a negative influence on her family's love inheritance. Even on his deathbed, he told Meredith's mother that she was a mistake and should never have been born. These words deeply impacted Meredith's mother, causing her to question her worth and value. As a result, she became a people-pleaser, always putting the needs of others before her own. This pattern was passed down to Meredith, who believed she had to give and sacrifice herself to feel worthy of love and attention. It's no coincidence that the man she picked also cheated on her.

It's a common trait among many, as we often try to please others to feel loved and valued. Once Meredith explored her past and realized the generational story that linked her circumstances, the spell was broken. She had the information she needed to become courageous and create boundaries.

Discovery Practice

To transform your love inheritance story, start by gaining awareness of what that story is. Explore your past and ask questions of your family members to uncover the truth about events that may shape your beliefs about love and relationships.

Your story may not be as apparent as Meredith's. Or maybe your parents are gone, and you have no uncles or aunts to give you information. There is still hope to discover your story. You have an inner knowing that you can access. Remember, everything you have gone through is in your mind's unconscious, subconscious, and preconscious levels. You can remember everything in your lineage.

Once you clearly understand your love inheritance story, you can begin the process of forgiveness, both for yourself and for any family members who may have contributed to your story negatively. With forgiveness, you can let go of any resentment or pain from the past and move forward with an open heart.

Forgiveness is not about letting the other person off the hook; it's about letting yourself off the hook. It's about understanding that everyone does the best they can with the tools and resources they have at the time. It's about understanding we all run on unconscious patterns that cause us to make mistakes and have flaws. So, if you're ready to rewrite your inherited love story by finding the truth, then start by asking questions. Remember to approach this with an explorer mindset.

CHAPTER 3

Find Forgiveness

According to Colin Tipping, *Radical Forgiveness* [14] is a process that helps people let go of anger, resentment, and other negative emotions that can prevent them from moving forward in their lives. The process involves acknowledging our role in our suffering and recognizing that the people who have hurt us have been our "teachers" who have helped us learn valuable lessons.

Tipping says we choose the people we interact with throughout our lives, including our parents, partners, and even strangers, to learn important lessons that help us evolve. These interactions and relationships teach us how to set boundaries, be more confident and assertive, and recognize and avoid manipulation and entanglement. While these choices are often made on a pre-conscious level, they serve a purpose in our personal growth and development. Be mindful that these choices are not made to seek pain or disrespect but rather to learn and grow. Even when we encounter people who cause us pain, we have chosen them to teach us something valuable.

When we forgive others, we forgive ourselves.

Becoming aware of and understanding this allows you to forgive them for putting themselves in this position of teaching. You also forgive yourself for picking this painful lesson. Forgiveness can be difficult when the pain is deep. But by now, I hope you are at a point in your journey to see that unless you release your pain story by forgiving, you will not be able to heal or be happy.

All Healing is Self-Healing

Radical Forgiveness was one of the first books I read on my journey to self-love. After a strained conversation with my third lawyer during my divorce, I was left feeling hurt and misunderstood when they blamed me for my ex's behavior. I felt like a victim all over again and left the office feeling powerless. The realization that I had a role in my suffering was difficult to accept.

It took me some time, but I eventually realized that forgiveness meant setting myself free. Forgiveness was not about the other person. It was about my inner peace and happiness. Holding onto resentment and anger toward someone else only caused suffering within myself.

Religious leaders and spiritual teachings have emphasized the importance of forgiveness for centuries, and I ultimately found that my desire for freedom surpassed my desire to be right. Learning to forgive was a crucial step in my journey to healing and liberation, and it's essential for you.

Forgiveness is a process, and it takes time. It did not happen overnight, but the more I practiced it, the more I realized its power to transform my life. It allowed me to let go of the past and move forward with a renewed sense of hope and freedom.

I also learned that forgiveness does not mean forgetting. It does not mean condoning or excusing the actions of others. It simply means letting go of the hurt and resentment and moving forward with love and understanding.

The practice of forgiveness can create a more loving and compassionate world for ourselves and those around us. Some steps that encourage forgiveness include:

1. **Acknowledge and validate your feelings:** Recognizing and acknowledging the pain and hurt you have experienced is essential. This may involve journaling, talking with a therapist or trusted friend, or simply sitting with and understanding your emotions.
2. **Practice self-compassion**: It can be easy to turn inward and blame ourselves when we have experienced harm or trauma. However, practicing self-compassion and understanding that we are human and prone to making mistakes is an important step in the forgiveness process.
3. **Set boundaries:** Setting healthy boundaries can help protect us from being re-traumatized or hurt again. This may involve limiting communication with the person who has caused you harm or creating physical or emotional distance.
4. **Let go of the need for revenge**: While it can be tempting to seek revenge or justice for the harm done, this can perpetuate the cycle of negativity and prevent healing. Instead, try to focus on letting go of this desire and finding ways to move forward positively.

5. **Express forgiveness**: This may involve writing a letter to the person central to your trauma, saying a prayer or mantra, or simply making the conscious decision to let go of the negative feelings and move forward.

There are many different approaches to forgiveness, and what works for one person may not work for another. Some people find it helpful to seek therapy or counseling to work through their feelings and learn how to forgive. Others find solace in prayer, meditation, writing in a journal, or talking to a trusted friend or family member. Whatever approach you choose, be open and willing to let go of the hurt. Through it all, remember to be patient and kind to yourself.

When it is Not Easy to Forgive

We sometimes can't seem to let go of the hurt and resentment. There is friction in the process of forgiving. If you are at this point in your journey, first, find comfort in the fact that resistance to forgiving is a natural response to pain and betrayal. It is the norm to find difficulty in letting go of negative feelings toward someone who has caused us harm. But remember that you are not doing this for them. You are doing this for yourself because you deserve to be free from the emotional burden of carrying these negative feelings.

The resistance may come because you feel it is unfair to let this person off the hook. But similarly, forgiveness is not about fairness or justice. You are not weak for letting go, either. In reality, forgiveness takes strength and courage. Its complexity means processing difficult emotions and memories. It may even require you to change your relationships or behavior.

You will become aware of the most profound understanding of your pain and realize that you can't possibly know all the reasons and scenarios that influenced how you got here in your life. But you can continue to understand that the more you embrace these practices, the closer you will come to the truth. Even without all the answers, you can move on from the pain. And releasing the old story of neediness, resentment, or betrayal can only be done through forgiveness. There's no other way.

Forgive Through Your Heart

The heart chakra, also known as the Anahata chakra in Sanskrit, is located at the center of the chest and is associated with the element of air - think Prana, Breath of Life. It is the fourth chakra in the seven-chakra system. It is responsible for our ability to give and receive love and our capacity for compassion, empathy, and connection with others. When the heart chakra is balanced, we feel open, loving, and compassionate towards ourselves and others, and we can connect with others in a deep and meaningful way. See Figure 3.

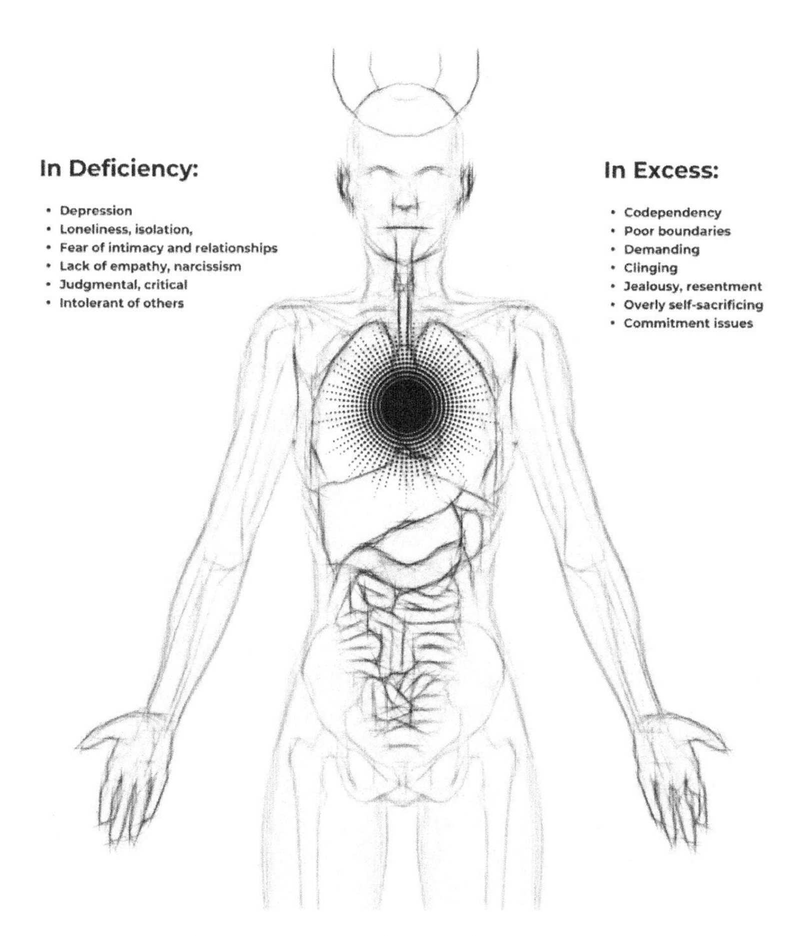

Figure 3. The Heart Chakra

However, when the heart chakra becomes blocked or unbalanced, it can lead to feelings of isolation, loneliness, and disconnection from others. Various factors, including unresolved past trauma, negative thought patterns, and a lack of self-love, can cause this. Another reason the heart chakra becomes blocked is a lack of forgiveness.

Holding on to grudges or resentment towards others can create a blockage in the heart chakra, preventing us from fully opening up to love and connection. Physical symptoms also manifest and can include chest pain, asthma, high blood pressure, heart problems, and immune system issues.

Forgiveness is a crucial aspect of healing and balancing the heart chakra, as it allows us to release any stuck hurt energy that may be causing a blockage. By practicing forgiveness, we open ourselves to the heart chakra's full potential, leading to inner peace, contentment, and a deeper connection with ourselves and others.

Other ways of freeing energy to the heart chakra include:

Practice the mantra YAM

In particular, the YAM mantra can open and balance the heart chakra. To practice this mantra, sit in a comfortable position with your spine straight and your eyes closed. Take a few deep breaths to relax and center yourself. Then, repeat the sound "yam" slowly and silently to yourself. You can also chant the mantra out loud if you prefer. As you repeat the mantra, focus your attention on the heart chakra. Visualize it as opening and healing.

Affirmations

Here are a few affirmations you can use to help open and balance your heart chakra:

- "I am worthy of love and respect."
- "I open my heart to give and receive love."
- "I am compassionate and understanding towards myself and others."

- "I am surrounded by love and positivity."
- "I let go of past hurts and embrace healing and forgiveness."

Remember to say these words with conviction and believe in them as you say them. Also, write them down and place them somewhere visible as a reminder to focus on their meaning throughout the day. Repeat these affirmations to yourself daily or whenever your heart chakra needs a boost.

Alternative practices

Additional practices you can employ include:

Meditation

Meditation can help calm the mind and focus on the present moment, which aids with opening the heart chakra. You can try a specific heart chakra meditation, focusing on the heart's energy and visualizing a glowing green light in the center of your chest.

Yoga

Yoga poses can open the chest and help to unblock the heart chakra. One such pose is the cobra pose or Bhujangasana in Sanskrit. Another pose is camel pose, also called Ustrasana in Sanskrit.

Crystalline Energy

Since the time of Plato, crystals have been known to resonate healing frequencies. You can wear them as jewelry or place them on your chest during meditation. Crystals such as rose quartz, green aventurine, and rhodonite are also helpful in this way.

Aromatherapy

Essential oils such as rose, jasmine, and sandalwood are great for heart opening. Use them in diffusers or apply them topically to your chest.

Psychotherapy

Psychotherapy (also called talk therapy) is a helpful tool for exploring patterns of codependency and unhealthy relationships and how they may be impacting the energy flow in your heart chakra. Standard techniques used to address these issues include:

1. Cognitive-behavioral therapy helps individuals identify and change negative thought patterns and behaviors.
2. Emotionally focused therapy focuses on helping individuals understand and express their emotions.
3. Dialectical behavior therapy is helpful for developing healthy coping skills and emotional regulation.
4. Mindfulness-based therapies can help individuals develop a non-judgmental awareness of their thoughts and emotions.
5. Group therapy involves participating in therapy sessions with others who struggle with similar issues. It is a helpful way to learn from others and gain support.

Breathwork

Breathing exercises can help open and activate the heart chakra. Breathwork techniques can also calm the nervous system and promote healing. My favorites include Holotropic Breathwork, Pranayama breathing as done in yoga, and Diaphragmatic breathing.

Heart-centered breathing also helps enable the flow of this chakra. To begin, sit comfortably with your spine straight and your hands resting on your knees. Close your eyes, and bring your awareness to your breath. As you inhale, visualize warm, glowing energy flowing into your heart chakra, and as you exhale, visualize that energy expanding outward to all parts of your body. Focus on your breath and the energy in your heart center for several minutes.

Laugh therapy

Laughter is a great way to invite positive energy into your life. When we laugh, we feel lighter and more positive, which can help to release any tension or blockages in the heart chakra. Some ways to incorporate laughter therapy into your daily routine include watching comedic movies or stand-up comedy routines and hanging out with friends who make you laugh. Get involved in activities that bring you happiness, such as dancing, singing, or playing sports. Also effective is laughter yoga, which involves simulated laughter and playful exercises.

Gratitude

Remember to practice mindfulness and gratitude. Focusing on the positive aspects of your life and expressing gratitude can shift your perspective to bring more joy into your heart.

Journaling

Journaling can be a helpful practice for opening the heart chakra because it allows you to explore and process your emotions and thoughts in a safe and private space. You can write about your feelings, past relationships, or anything else that comes to mind. Journaling is an individualized practice, and there is no right or wrong way to do it. The important thing is to take the time to explore your emotions and thoughts in a way that feels authentic and meaningful to you.

Forgiveness Raises Your Vibration

Every thought you have creates an energetic response expressed through your words, actions, and presence. They have a powerful impact on your life and all the world around you.

When you focus on positive thoughts and emotions, you can raise the vibration of your energy and attract more positivity into your life. On the other hand, negative thoughts and feelings can lower your vibration and attract negative experiences, as we've explored. The entire universe is energy that connects all sentient beings. This energetic connection explains why we can sometimes sense when someone is upset or angry even if they are not physically present with us.

As an intuitive person, you are sensitive to the energy of others. When you start vibrating at a higher frequency, you will naturally repel lower vibrations, and they will no longer affect you. You can practice blocking the vibration, but a more effective approach is to transform it through the power of forgiveness and the energy of your heart chakra.

When you begin by discovering your inherited love story and find the cracks in this foundation, you will have the information you need to start patching up those emotional blocks to self-love. It always beings with awareness. Remember, this is an exploratory journey.

The next stop on your journey to self-love is Step #2 - Self-Acceptance.

STEP #2

Clean Your House (Self-Acceptance)

As I began to love myself,
I found that anguish and emotional suffering
are warning signs that I was living
against my own truth.
Today I know this as authenticity.
Charlie Chaplin.

CHAPTER 4

Clean Body, Clean Mind

It is prevalent for people to struggle with self-acceptance and self-worth in today's world. The societal standards of beauty and acceptance can be challenging to live up to, and it's easy to feel like we are not enough if we don't fit into these narrow definitions. Oh yes, this is political.

Our response to these pressures can lead to self-destructive behaviors such as disordered eating and other harmful coping mechanisms like substance abuse. When we journey to self-love, we must stop at the kitchen and address how we treat our bodies because this affects all women (and some men) at any age.

Icon, Jane Fonda revealed in an Elle Magazine article [14] that she struggled with Bulimia most of her life and only overcame it in her 40s. Now in her 80's, Jane confesses, "I have to work every day to be self-accepting. It doesn't come easy to me." Jane's story illustrates that it's never too late to work on self-acceptance and self-worth. It's a journey that requires ongoing effort and self-reflection, but the rewards are immeasurable.

By learning to love and accept ourselves, we can find greater happiness and fulfillment in our lives and be better equipped to handle the challenges that come our way. And as Charlie Chaplin reminds us, the key to finding love and acceptance is first to recognize that emotional suffering means that you are living against your own truth. By facing these challenges and working through them, we can learn to love ourselves and live more authentic, fulfilling lives.

The "Not Good Enough" Culture

As demonstrated in Step #1, genetic makeup plays a significant role in how we process information and how we process stress. For example, some people are more prone to anxiety or depression due to genetic predisposition. Additionally, certain genetic variations affect the brain's functioning and its ability to process and retain information. Similarly, our bodies also have different ways of responding to stress, and our genetics can influence this.

Some people have a higher stress tolerance and can handle it better, while others are more prone to experiencing adverse effects of stress on their physical and mental health. Therefore, it is essential to be aware of your unique genetic makeup and how it impacts your processing of information and stress, and take steps to manage these factors to maintain optimal physical and mental health. Genetics is just one factor among many that can influence how we process information and treat our bodies. Another such factor is societal influence.

Females have a long history of being judged based on their physical appearance, dating back to the caveman era (I'm guessing) when women were selected for their ability to breed and bear children. Physical characteristics such as big hips and strong legs were indicative of a good "breeder." These same selection markers can still be seen in modern culture, with celebrities like Marilyn Monroe still adored for her hourglass figure. Even today, women continue to face pressure to conform to specific beauty standards.

The damaging effects on self-esteem and overall well-being are discussed, yet our culture continues to judge and evaluate women based on their physical appearance and sexual attractiveness. It seems like a never-ending battle for women. When they downplay their looks, the backlash is ugly, with insults and many other forms of abuse. Some women may be ostracized or excluded from social groups or activities because they are considered unattractive. Others face discrimination in the workplace because they do not conform to corporate beauty standards.

In many cases, this has resulted in missed promotions, lower pay, or other forms of workplace bias. There are even instances when women have difficulty finding romantic partners or maintaining relationships because of this. Yet playing into their attractiveness has made many women the target of sexual assault or harassment.

We are rising above this way of thinking to empower women. The *Me Too* movement is a social movement against sexual harassment and assault that gained widespread attention and support in 2017, especially on social media. It was started in 2006 by Tarana Burke, an American social activist, to help survivors of sexual violence, particularly young women of color from low-wealth communities, and to empower them to speak out about their experiences.

The movement gained international recognition in 2017 when the hashtag #MeToo was used on social media to help demonstrate the widespread prevalence of sexual harassment, especially in the workplace. The movement has inspired similar campaigns around the world, including the #BalanceTonPorc ("Expose Your Pig") movement in France and the #Niunamenos ("Not One Less") movement in Argentina.

Despite the efforts of the *Me Too* movement to expose and combat this, these harmful and objectifying ways of thinking about women are still deeply ingrained in our society, impacting the way women see themselves and how others treat them. We see this in the way women are portrayed in media and advertising and in the proliferation of apps and filters that allow for altering their appearance.

This constant pressure to conform to a certain standard of beauty leads to unhealthy behaviors like the obsession with diet and exercise or the use of cosmetics and plastic surgery to try to meet these unrealistic standards. Furthermore, focusing on appearance can distract us from other important aspects of ourselves, such as our character, intelligence, and talents.

Trying to Fill the Void

The most deadly and insidious way that many women often unwittingly reveal their unhappiness caused by this pressure is how they treat their bodies with food. Food has become a way of controlling to either punish or reward ourselves. We deprive ourselves of the nutrients we need and then binge on unhealthy foods to cope with our emotions. This cycle of restriction and bingeing can lead to serious health problems such as eating disorders and malnutrition.

According to the *National Eating Disorders Association* (NEDA) [16], women are more likely to develop an eating disorder than men. Here are some key statistics about eating disorders in women in the United States:

- Approximately 20 million women in the U.S. will have an eating disorder at some point in their lives.
- Women with eating disorders have a higher mortality rate than any other mental illness.
- Women who have experienced trauma or abuse are more likely to develop an eating disorder.
- The most common eating disorders are anorexia nervosa, bulimia nervosa, and binge eating disorder.
- About 50% of people with eating disorders meet the criteria for depression.
- Eating disorders often co-occur with other mental health conditions, such as anxiety, substance abuse, and personality disorders.
- The average age of onset for an eating disorder is 18-21. However, eating disorders can develop at any age and affect people of all genders, ages, and body sizes.

According to the National Association of Anorexia Nervosa and Associated Disorders (ANAD) [17], about 30 million people in the U.S. of all ages and genders suffer from an eating disorder. Every 62 minutes, at least one person dies as a direct result of an eating disorder. These disorders have the highest mortality rate of any mental illness. In Canada, eating disorders affect ten times more women than men. At any given time, 70% of women and 35% of men are on a diet.

Binge Eating Disorder (BED) is also prevalent in our society and is culturally accepted and promoted through the "super-size me" and all-you-can-eat restaurant culture. BED is three times more common than anorexia and Bulimia combined and is more common than breast cancer and HIV.

The CDC highlighted another troubling contributing factor to many women's negative association with food. Studies say that the negative experiences and trauma of Adverse Childhood Experiences (ACEs) [18] experienced by an individual during their childhood can have long-lasting effects on their health and well-being.

These ACES can manifest in various ways, including weight gain as a coping mechanism for depression, anxiety, and fear. The study found that adults with ACE exposure often had worse mental and physical health and poorer life outcomes. The study found that over 90% of women had high ACE exposure, influencing their self-perception and relationships in addition to their overall health and well-being.

Jenny's Story

Jenny reached out to me for help after the 14-year relationship with her common-law partner ended. Unexpectedly, on their anniversary, he proclaimed that he no longer wanted to be in a relationship. The sudden breakup left her homeless resulting in her living with her sister in another city. When Jenny came to me, she was newly diagnosed with diabetes, clinically obese, and had started taking high blood pressure medication.

She felt alone and unsupported in her grief over the relationship that took up more than a decade of her life. Her family expected her to "just ignore her heartbreak and move on." Her sister even stopped having meals with her and barely talked to her.

This lack of support and acceptance of grief is unfortunately common in society. We are expected to suppress our feelings and find distractions instead of allowing ourselves to process and heal thoroughly. Jenny had buried her feelings in food.

Working with me, she improved her diet and addressed her underlying love patterns. As a result, Jenny lost weight, lowered her risk of obesity and diabetes, and eventually stopped taking her high blood pressure medication. She said, "I didn't think I could feel like this again. You took every piece of my life and fixed it."

True Beauty Starts on the Inside

The Jenny who first came to me would not have been able to make such a bold statement. She was on the verge of hopelessness. And what Jenny learned is that wherever you are on your journey, now is the perfect time to turn your life around.

I present to you the same truth – you can make the bold changes needed to take control of your physical health so that you feel secure in how you look and feel.

I understand how difficult it is to love ourselves as we are when we get signals from everywhere telling us that we aren't good enough. But, first and foremost, I urge you to recognize that these societal messages and beauty standards do not represent your true worth or value as an individual. Take your focus away from these messages and place it on your self-care and self-love rather than trying to conform to external expectations.

Once, when I was in Berlin chatting with a woman after a hot yoga class, I asked if there was a beauty salon in the area that did eyelash extensions. Blank stares met my eyes. Then a U.S. Expat woman stepped forward and said, "Oh, they don't take care of themselves like we do back home."

At first, I was surprised. But I took a beat and realized how European culture embraced healthy rather than superficial beauty. That was a big 'aha' moment because it led to me no longer wearing those extensions. And it was a catalyst that had me reviewing the things I did to my body and why.

Beauty is an inside game. It's not just about appearances but about feeling good inside and out. Loving yourself is reflected in how you treat your body. When we constantly alter our appearance to fit societal standards of beauty, we exhaust and ultimately damage our mental and physical health. By loving ourselves as we are, we can focus on caring for ourselves healthily rather than trying to fit an idealized image.

Respect and kindness become the mantra for caring for our bodies. We are sure to nourish it with healthy food, stay hydrated, get enough sleep, and engage in physical activity that feels good to us. Treat your body right, and you will feel more confident and optimistic, thus arming yourself with the tools to navigate the challenges and stressors of life better.

A clean body is a clean mind. And a clean mind leads to more confidence and comfort in your skin and increases your sense of self-love. Let's dive deeper into the mind-body connection.

The Connection Between Mind and Body

Physiologically, the brain and peripheral nervous system (the parts of the nervous system that are outside of the brain and spinal cord), the endocrine and immune systems, all the organs of your body, and all your emotional responses share a common chemical language. Whereas you and I use words and text, this language results from the release of neurotransmitters. Neurons facilitate this language by sending and receiving electrical signals. This process allows the brain to control the body's actions and reactions. This complex and constant communication happens whether you are asleep or awake.

Our body is the barometer for our emotional well-being.

This communication is called the mind-body connection. In a phrase, the mind-body connection is how our mental and emotional states affect our physical health and vice versa.

Before we delve deeper into the workings of the mind-body connection, we must make a significant distinction. The words "mind" and "brain" are not interchangeable. The mind includes mental states such as thoughts, emotions, beliefs, attitudes, and images, while the brain serves as the physical mechanism that enables us to experience these mental states. Mental states can be conscious or unconscious. Emotional reactions to situations can occur without our awareness of the cause. Each mental state has a corresponding physiological impact. For instance, anxiety triggers the release of stress hormones.

The concept of a connection between the mind and body has been around for a while. Historically, almost every system of medicine around the world treated the mind and body as a unified entity. However, in the 17th century, the Western world shifted the view of the mind and body as separate units. This perspective viewed the body as a machine with replaceable and independent parts without connection to the mind. While this Western viewpoint led to advances in surgery, trauma care, pharmaceuticals, and other areas of allopathic medicine, it also limited research into the emotional and spiritual aspects of human life. It downplayed the body's ability to heal itself.

In the 20th century, this perspective shifted once more as researchers resumed the study of the mind-body connection and scientifically established the complex connections between the mind and body.

The HPA Axis

One key player in the mind-body connection is the hypothalamic-pituitary-adrenal (HPA) axis. This complex system helps regulate the body's response to stress by releasing the stress hormone cortisol. Feelings of hopelessness and helplessness caused by stressful situations exacerbate the body's stress response leading to chronic activation of the HPA axis. On the other hand, positive attitudes and coping mechanisms, such as mindfulness, have the opposite effect.

See Figure 4.

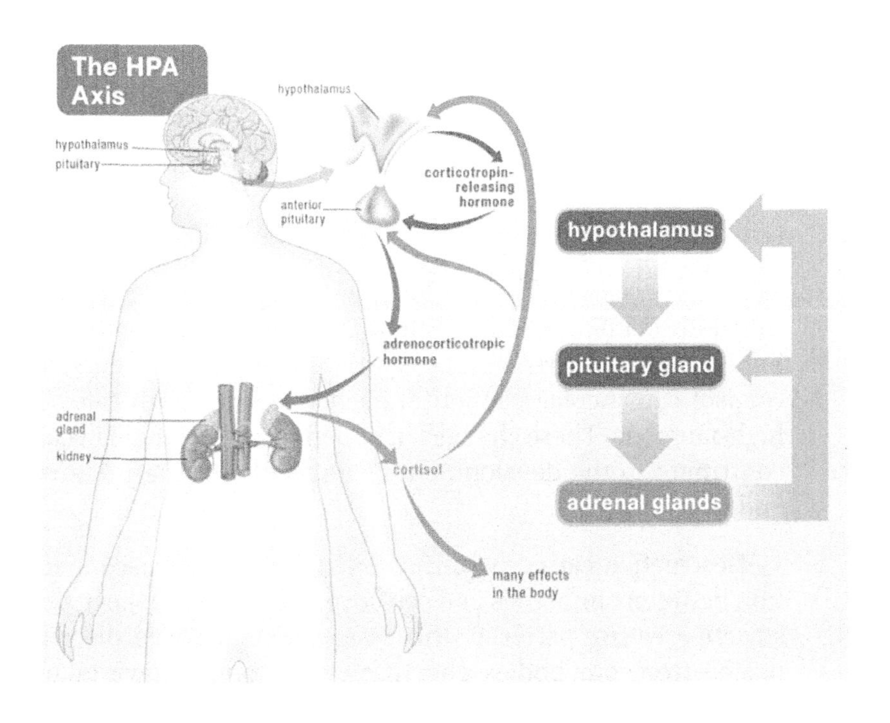

Figure 4. The Hypothalamus, Pituitary, Adrenal Axis

The HPA axis helps regulate hunger, metabolism, and mood as well. When we are in the Sympathetic (fight or flight) response, the system activates the systems that are needed, such as the brain and muscles. As a result, our digestive system gets shut down. When we use food to cope with stressful situations, our body doesn't do a good job digesting it.

Disruptions in this system lead to a wide range of health issues, including eating disorders, in addition to contributing to the development of several physical and psychological symptoms such as anxiety, depression, and changes in appetite and metabolism. As mentioned earlier, eating disorders such as anorexia nervosa, bulimia nervosa, and binge eating disorder often start as coping mechanisms to deal with overwhelming emotions. These behaviors provide a temporary sense of control and calm, but over time, they become ingrained and difficult to change.

Additionally, studies [19] show that high cortisol levels are linked to a higher risk of obesity and metabolic disorders, as cortisol can increase appetite, particularly for high-calorie, high-fat foods. These changes in appetite and metabolism can contribute to the development of unhealthy eating patterns and weight gain.

Destructive eating patterns contribute to the disconnection between our bodies and self-love. When we engage in destructive eating patterns, this is a sign that we've disconnected from our bodies and that our emotions have taken over. Feelings of guilt and shame undermine our sense of self-worth and promote a negative body image. Then the cycle of negative self-perception and disordered eating behaviors is created.

Physical healing by engaging in healthy eating habits is an essential step in promoting emotional healing. Caring for our physical body makes us feel more in control of our lives and leads to a more positive self-image. Additionally, engaging in regular physical activity and exercise can also be beneficial for emotional healing. Physical activity [20] helps reduce symptoms of depression and anxiety, improves self-esteem, and promotes feelings of well-being. When we move, stuck energy gets released—more in the next chapter.

Breaking the cycle of disordered eating means addressing underlying emotional issues and learning new coping mechanisms. The key is reframing our view of ourselves and our bodies by learning to accept it as it is. Treating our bodies positively with food brings us to a place of balance, harmony, and happiness. It is challenging to reach this place, especially in the Western world.

In North America, processed foods are highly marketed and available in huge quantities. These foods are high in sugar, salt, and unhealthy fats. They are also typically addictive due to their palatability and convenience. And they are not designed to keep you healthy and strong but to promote addiction.

The companies that manufacture these foods spend billions of dollars to ensure they achieve the Bliss Point. Bliss Point [21] is used in the food industry to refer to the optimal level of sweetness, saltiness, and fat factor that will make a food or beverage most appealing to consumers. The idea is to create food that is so appealing that people will want to eat more than they should. Food companies use various techniques, such as flavor chemistry and food engineering, to create irresistible products which trigger overeating. Excessive food consumption is another goal of achieving Bliss Point.

Many of us turn to processed foods as a source of emotional comfort. That is why we call them “comfort food.” These foods stimulate the release of pleasure-inducing chemicals in the brain, such as endorphins. They provide a temporary sense of calm or happiness. However, these foods also contribute to inflammation, other health problems, and negative feelings. When caught in the cycle of using food to comfort ourselves, we begin by identifying the emotions or situations that trigger negative eating behaviors, such as stress, boredom, or sadness, and then learn new coping mechanisms to manage these emotions.

The most significant resistance I found in my nutrition practice was taking away the toxic food. Whenever I mentioned an Elimination Diet, I would get much descent. So instead, I enlisted clients to focus on eating an abundance of good clean food instead. Here, in particular, we must ramp up our practice of loving kindness toward ourselves and only give more of the good and not focus on taking away toxic food energy.

Another critical aspect of "house cleaning" is to make sure your environment when you eat is calm and joyful. Replace pro-inflammatory foods with healthier and more natural options that provide physical and emotional nourishment. Consume a variety of nutrient-dense foods. And practice moderation with portion sizes.

Our bodies thrive physically and emotionally when our "house" is clean. And a clean house needs to be cleared of pro-inflammatory foods like processed foods, sugar, and saturated fats. Such foods were created to keep you hooked and unhappy.

When you finally break this cycle of unhealthy emotional eating, you will, over time, find it easier to resist the pro-inflammatory foods. Approach the change with a non-restrictive and non-punishing mindset. So, instead of placing strict rules and limits on yourself, focus on progress, not perfection. It's okay to slip up and make mistakes. We all do it, and it's an integral part of the process. With this mindset, you can do what Jenny did in no time.

At this juncture, I want to remind you that you are doing so well. Reach out for support any time by emailing us at support@dianamikas.com.

CHAPTER 5

Elevate Your Energy

Emotions are a form of energy. Like any other form of energy, like solar or wind energy, they are powerful, so much so that they drive our thoughts, behaviors, and actions. Emotions are a complex mix of physiological and psychological responses to certain stimuli, ranging from the positive end of the spectrum with examples like happiness and joy to the negative end with emotions like anger and fear. You can't experience these powerful emotions in only one dimension, which is why emotions affect us physically and mentally. Physically, emotions change our heart rate, breathing, and muscle tension. Mentally, emotions manifest through thoughts and feelings.

Different emotions emit different energy frequencies. Positive emotions such as love and joy give off higher frequencies. Alternatively, negative emotions such as fear and anger have lower frequencies. When we are sad or heartbroken, we say, "I feel low" or "I feel blue." These are perfect descriptions of the frequency of energy felt as our energy tanks feel depleted. A classic symptom of this is difficulty finding the motivation or stamina to engage in activities or to interact with others.

Sadness and other negative emotions can also affect our perception of the world and ourselves, leading to negative thoughts and self-image, further contributing to low energy and lack of motivation, creating an unhelpful cycle of unlove. We call this the Heart Armouring effect previously mentioned.

When we are in a state of armoring our hearts, we block our love energy from getting out, and we stop love energy from getting in. You will also filter all experiences through your inherited love stories. Imagine you're in the "Cone of Silence." Only the cone is like a fine filter. The big emotions like anger, resentment, mistrust, and fear keep bouncing around within the cone. The more nuanced feelings of anxiety, codependency, passive aggression and undertones of fear are seeping out, only to be reflected back to you in the form of relationships.

During a relationship, you engage in an energetic exchange. When the relationship ends, you need to clear the other person's energy from your space and reclaim your energy from them. Release yourself from this cycle of unloving yourself and separate the bonds that keep your energy intertwined with the toxic person or event with energy healing. The process allows you to establish a stronger sense of self in the present and focus less on the past relationship.

How do we achieve higher frequencies of the positive emotional energy that sustains our sense of self-love? Let's review the steps outlined in the Anatomy of heartbreak and the practices that will shift your energy.

Healing a Broken Heart on an Energetic Level

Not a big fan of staying in heartbreak, I encourage you to notice what's keeping you in sadness. Are you going through a breakup, divorce, or loss of some kind?

These events are part of the human condition that we all must go through so we can evolve. These complex and traumatic experiences cause various emotions like grief and depression that we don't like to experience.

For example, the end of a relationship is a time of change. It means the loss of shared plans and dreams for the future and a sense of identity and self-worth. The ordeal makes you want to lock your heart up and throw away the key so that no one ever gets close enough to hurt you in such a way again. But you can't fully open yourself to self-love without your heart. It is the origin of powerful emotion and drives our decisions.

In many ways, the reason that your heart continues to feel broken and so very tender is that you're holding on to the experience. In your mind, you are replaying the events that transpired, thereby repeatedly breaking your heart. Just like when a relationship ends and material belongings are returned, a similar process needs to occur on an energetic level.

You are the wounded healer.

Energy healing is a holistic practice that works with the subtle aspects of your being. It acknowledges that you are more than just your physical self and that you are energy. When this energy flows freely, you experience health and well-being on all levels. However, sometimes this energy can become blocked or stagnant, resulting in emotional and physical pain.

Recreate the free flow of energy through your heart by systematically going through the anatomy of your heartbreak and stimulating transformation at each level. You will have pitfalls, so pull out your self-compassion and buffer the impact. For this next part refer to Figure 1 – Anatomy of Heartbreak.

Shock and Trauma

Social rejection, including romantic rejection, significantly impacts the body and mind. It activates the sympathetic nervous system and initiates the fight or flight response. The body goes into defense mode. The heart starts pumping blood quickly. The brain becomes hyperactive, looking for sources of danger. The muscles are tense, ready to react to this danger. The parts of your body not involved in this response shut down so that all energy and resources are diverted to maintain this reaction to keep you safe and alive.

When this stress response is activated repeatedly or for prolonged periods, it weakens you mentally and physically. And when you're stuck in this phase, it's like being in a car accident every single day – doomed to repeat the same trauma over and over again.

The Awareness:

Become aware of your desire to shut down. Understandably, you would want to suppress these emotions out of fear of their intensity. We also shut down because we want to avoid feeling the pain that comes with rejection. However, such actions only make you feel worse. Blocking these emotions prevents healing and moving on because they get lodged in the energetic field. Like the wall of a dam, suppression and avoidance stifle energy flow to and from your heart.

The Antidote:

We tend to hold our breath when in shock, which shuts down oxygen flow to the brain, impairing our ability to think critically. Instead, do deep belly breaths from your diaphragm. Inhale for a count of four, hold your breath for four, then release on four and hold for four. This "box" breathing technique will quickly relax your nervous system taking you out of the Sympathetic (fight or flight) state and back to the Parasympathetic (rest and digest).

Anger and Denial

Our society is more accepting of men showing anger than women. We are often publicly criticized and ridiculed for showing anger. So, we do our best to shove this emotion down, causing more energetic blocks. What if, instead, we considered anger to be a dear friend rather than an enemy?

Anger serves as the primary emotional state that upholds our boundaries. It indicates that something is wrong, a boundary has been crossed, or a need is not being met. Anger is also the appropriate response to oppression. Like any other natural emotion, anger deserves to be honored. It is valid. Our choice lies in what we do with that emotion.

The Awareness:

Do not embrace aggression. The two are distinct emotions with different meanings and implications. Anger is a natural and normal emotion that signals that something is wrong and action needs to be required to address the situation. On the other hand, aggression is an action or behavior done to harm or intimidate others. It is a destructive reaction to anger. While anger can be an appropriate and healthy response that leads to healing, aggression is not. Recognize the difference between the two and productively channel anger instead of resorting to aggressive behavior.

The Antidote:

Slow the situation down and be still. Like in Seinfeld, when George's father yells, "Serenity Now." Or the Mel Robbins technique of counting backward from 5. Take a beat.

Only then can you listen to the message of the anger and identify what boundaries need re-establishing. You will see the situation more clearly with compassion for yourself and others.

Denial and Isolation

When you find yourself unable to move on from a relationship and constantly check your ex's social media status, it is a sign that you're in denial about the end of the relationship. Seeing their face triggers a response in the brain similar to a drug craving or high, making you feel like you're still in love. However, seeing the evidence that the relationship is genuinely over also activates the area of the brain responsible for behavioral adjustments, leading to the realization that it's time to unfollow or unfriend them.

As you move on, you may feel isolated and disconnected from your social group, particularly if your friends are part of couple relationships. Your friend circle might get small, further reinforcing your feelings of isolation. Remember, this is just a temporary condition on your journey to self-love. Soon, your progesterone levels will rise, which can increase the desire to seek out new social connections.

The Awareness:

Stagnation and wallowing in self-pity are the enemies here. They are no longer part of your new high-vibe life. Take practical steps to move on by taking control of your energy and unfollowing, blocking, or removing them from your social media. Like ripping off a band-aid, it's painful but necessary.

The Antidote:

Focus your energy on connecting with people you like and who positively uplift you. One day, you'll suddenly notice that the people you meet are more encouraging and optimistic. It's a sign that you're on your way to the higher resonance of attraction. You'll feel hopeful and encouraged to put yourself out there again.

Understanding this framework and what stage you are currently at does not make the pain magically go away. After all, the healing process is multi-faceted and requires various forms of support. What this knowledge does do is take you one step closer to increasing the frequency of your energy.

How Jenny went from Low to High Vibe

The emotional pain from feeling rejected and dismissed by her family weighed on her heavily. It manifested in the physical symptoms associated with metabolic syndrome. Metabolic Syndrome [22] is a group of risk factors that increase a person's chances of developing heart disease, diabetes, and stroke. These risk factors include high blood pressure, high blood sugar, excess body fat around the waist, and abnormal cholesterol levels.

The low frequencies generated by her pain led to inflammation throughout her body. Through the process of addressing and healing these emotional issues, Jenny experienced a shift from heavy to light feelings. Incorporating changes in diet and exercise also contributed to her overall improvement in health. Jenny reported feeling a renewed sense of well-being and self-confidence. She said, "I didn't think I could feel this way again."

Rethink Your Perception of Your Energy

A scientific study [23] highlights the powerful impact emotions have on a person's energy levels. Expressing negative emotions leads to feelings of fatigue and low energy. Feeling positive emotions, on the other hand, increases energy levels and overall well-being. Emotions influence the body's production of dopamine, serotonin, and norepinephrine. These chemicals regulate mood as well as motivation and energy. Low levels of these neurotransmitters cause feelings of depression and low energy.

Physical exercise, known to release endorphins and other feel-good chemicals in the brain, helps improve mood and energy levels. Regular exercise reduces stress, improves sleep, and promotes overall physical fitness, all of which contribute to increased energy levels.

A systematic review and meta-analysis of 15 prospective studies [24], including more than 2 million person-years, found that regular physical activity is associated with a lower risk of depression. The research suggests that the relationship between physical activity and depression is non-linear, with the most significant risk reduction seen at lower levels of physical activity. Specifically, adults who met physical activity recommendations, equivalent to 2.5 hours per week of brisk walking, had a lower risk of depression compared with adults who reported no physical activity.

The most beneficial type of exercise for reducing the risk of depression is moderate-intensity aerobic exercise, such as brisk walking, cycling, or swimming. There is a delicate balance between exercising and listening to your body's needs. Over-exercising leads to more stress in the body and increased cortisol levels. So be aware.

Gentle exercises such as walking, yoga, and (my favorite) Tai Chi are known for calming the nervous system and aiding in energy elevation. These exercises are low-impact and can easily be incorporated into your daily routine. They also go a long way in helping you accept your body and life as they are.

Release Trauma from Your Body

Exercise plays a role in releasing tension from your system. And there's a growing awareness of the role of fascia and how it is a significant player in releasing trauma.

Fascial release is a type of manual therapy that focuses on releasing tension and restrictions in the connective tissue that surrounds and permeates muscles, organs, and other structures in the body. The fascia is a web-like structure that connects and supports the body. When it becomes tight or restricted, it can create areas of congestion, leading to pain, discomfort, and impaired movement.

This type of therapy treats many conditions, including chronic pain, muscle tension, restricted mobility, and postural imbalances, and most importantly can release trauma. It is considered a holistic approach and complements other forms of therapy, such as physical therapy, chiropractic, and osteopathy. And it elevates your energy levels quickly.

I'm obsessed with fascia release techniques because they're easy and quickly get to the stuck energy causing the problems. Even if you have no awareness of any restrictions, doing a daily practice of maneuvers will reveal them.

By releasing tension and holding in the fascia, the body's energy can flow more freely, improving energy levels. Do this by focusing on releasing tension in the areas of the body that hold a lot of stress, such as the neck, shoulders, and back. Traditionally, this can be done using tools such as foam rollers, massage balls, or hands-on therapy. You can also focus on releasing tension in the areas associated with the body's energy centers, such as the feet, legs, and hips, as well as the chest and abdominal area.

Breathe deeply and relax as much as possible during the process. Fascial release should be done gently and slowly. It's best to start small sessions and gradually increase the duration and intensity. Fascial release is an excellent addition to your self-care toolkit along your journey to self-love.

Co-founder of a non-profit initiative called Human Garage [25], Garry Lineham, says,

"Let's think of our entire body as a computer rather than the brain. The brain processes information and presents it so that the user, us, can understand. Every moment of our life is recorded by the computer and stored in the fascia. The fascia has a brain, and itself is called the interstitium, which is 1000 times more powerful than our human brain.

Trauma comes with an action which is physical, emotional, or perceptual and a reaction which is physical. When the body is in stress, and physical release of this process is compromised, trauma is then stored in the body. Trauma can be as simple as your parents forgetting you as a child at the mall. That feeling propagates as we get older, and "we're not..."

feeling comes up. We have the same processing or programs that run even as an adult.

Movement is the cure for all things in the body, and the origin of movement is BREATH. If we are not breathing, we are not alive, and this is where all functional dysfunction starts. By moving the body through all ranges of motion, we are preparing the computer so that it has a recall and the ability to process the information. In order to release trauma, the body needs serotonin, which comes from the small intestine. Serotonin makes us feel connected to the world and allows what seems like an acute trauma or a pain to be understood by the user, us again. Trauma is simply information that is stuck in the body. Nothing more, nothing less."

The beauty of trauma release through fascial maneuvers is that you can do these yourself without the need for a practitioner. It is safe because the movements are gentle and subtle, with no adverse effects other than the release of the stuck energy in the body. My releases come in the form of hot flashes when I do fascial maneuvers. Garry says, "It's Ok to burp or fart."

Energy Elevation Starts With The Mind

The second universal law, known as the law of vibration, states that everything in the universe is in constant motion and vibrates at a specific frequency. This frequency is called vibrational energy. The only difference between one object and another is the rate of its vibrations. This energy, whether from a person, physical space, or group of people, cannot be seen nor touched. Yet, we can sense, feel, react to, and interact with it.

The most beautiful thing about this law of the universe is that rates of vibration are not fixed. We all have a unique vibrational frequency. Some people have higher rates of vibration than others. At any time, we can adjust our vibration. See Figure 5.

Stage	Emotion	State	Wholeness Scale
Control	Confident	Grounded	80 -100%
Calibration	Assured	Correction	70 -80%
Acceptance	Calm	Composure	50 - 70%
Abandonment	Depressed	Isolation	30 - 50%
Loss	Sad	Denial	15 - 30%
Grief	Shock	Panic	0 - 15%

High ↑ Low

Figure 5. Emotional Energy Vibration Scale

So, when you feel you are in a low vibrational scenario, it's a matter of acting to increase the frequency. The key is to become more attuned to your energy. The greater the awareness, the more you see how your vibes affect your entire experience.

Our energy responds to our frame of mind, thoughts, and beliefs. Our views and opinions create a specific frequency or vibration that directly impacts our energy levels. Thoughts are electric. Their impulses are the result of the firing of neurons in the brain. On the other hand, emotions are the magnetic aspect of our being. They create a magnetic field around us, and we feel their physiological and energetic characteristics throughout the body. They result from the release of hormones and chemicals in the body.

The law of attraction states that we attract into our lives whatever we focus on, whether it's positive or negative. Focusing on positive thoughts and feelings will attract positive experiences and energy into our lives. Focusing on negative thoughts and emotions will attract negative experiences and energy into our lives, .

The same philosophy applies to the energy vibrations we have. When our energy is high and positive, we tend to be more attractive to others and to the things we desire in life as we vibrate at a similar frequency. Conversely, when our energy is low and negative, we tend to repel others and the things we desire, as we are vibrating at a different frequency.

How does the law of vibration differ from the law of attraction? Both are similar, and they even work together. Understanding and utilizing the law of vibration is necessary for the law of attraction to work in your favor. The law of vibration is about matching the frequency of what you desire, while the law of attraction is about creating that frequency within yourself. Work with both laws to align your vibration with what you want to attract.

To use the law of attraction to your advantage and to elevate your energy, it's essential to understand where you are in your energy journey and take steps to release sadness and past traumas that may be holding you back.

CHAPTER 6

Fill Your Space

Our perception of reality and whether we feel confident starts in our brains. Its complex network of around 100 billion neurons makes it the most incredible supercomputer on earth. It is adept at processing and organizing information and functions at a very high speed, with trillions of electric pulses passing through it every second. This network encodes and stores memories and experiences, which make up the unique individual that you are. These processes flow effortlessly on a regular day when all is fine and dandy.

But when a traumatic event happens, this system gets disrupted, altering memory storage processes and changing the brain's physical structure. The effects are long-lasting.[26] Trauma is not just an emotional or mental experience. It leaves a physical imprint on the body. Like a festering wound, trauma weakens the body's defenses, manifests as illness, and changes your physiology and how you hold it all together.

The impact that trauma has on your life is called emotional baggage. It feels like a physical weight that prevents you from moving forward. While everyone carries unprocessed emotions to some degree, these unprocessed feelings affect your self-perception, reactions to stress, physical well-being, and relationships with others.

This situation supports the mind-body connection because mental and emotional health impacts physical health. Trapped emotions result in several physical ailments, and muscle tension is a common complaint. More precisely, trauma causes stress, which activates the fight or flight response, and muscle tension arises as a way to protect the body. We see this in body posture, such as holding the chin close to the chest, slouching, and hunching. Additionally, it contributes to feelings of insecurity, guilt, shame, or powerlessness. So, we tend to make our bodies smaller as if we want to be invisible.

Releasing trauma from your body changes your posture. You will sit up straighter and stand with your shoulders back and your chest out. Your head will be held high. Your body language will be open and relaxed, and inviting. Making eye contact with other people will feel easy and seamless.

You will nonverbally communicate to all around you that you are confident and sure of yourself. This confidence will further activate a belief in yourself and your abilities. You'll have greater self-esteem and a more positive image of yourself. You'll be more likely to take risks and try new things to achieve personal growth and fulfillment.

This chapter is dedicated to molding that image of you by shifting the weight of the emotional baggage you have accumulated over the years through your body.

Shape Who You Want to Become

It's apparent when observing a person if they possess confidence or not. A confident person stands tall with a straight back, an open chest, and a level head. They don't shy away from interacting with new individuals and can effortlessly speak in front of a group. They assert themselves and establish boundaries without feeling guilty. Remember the attributes of a Secure Attachment Style mentioned in Chapter 2?

A secure person has mindful self-compassion. They accept their faults and understand that all humans suffer from self-criticism. They also know that the path to becoming the best person means making lots of mistakes. And when we are kind to ourselves, we are more open to learning what these mistakes offer us. As if you are speaking to a child who made a mistake. Instantly you can see how they change their body posture from small to bigger when they've been vindicated.

You might not be that person right now, but you are on your way.

Start by observing how your posture shifts when you feel insecure or low in self-esteem. Your body posture may be closed, indicated by crossed arms or legs to create a barrier between yourself and others. You might round your shoulders as if to guard your heart.

Making eye contact is difficult. The eyes are the windows to the soul, and they reveal so much that you might want to hide. When you shield yourself in this way, it can be misinterpreted as a sign of dishonesty or weakness, creating even more distance between you and others who might otherwise offer support in challenging times.

Your insecurity may manifest in your posture in other ways. Do you fidget, displaying nervous movements like tapping your feet, playing with your hair, or twisting objects? Maybe you shift your weight from foot to foot when uncomfortable or anxious?

Do you often give off a submissive demeanor with a low head position? Do you try to take less space by shrinking your body so that you are not a bother to other people or do not attract attention?

Low self-confidence is not a personality trait. Rather, it is a state of mind and is linked to the health of your Solar Plexus Chakra. When you notice self-limiting beliefs and harsh self-talk, nip the negativity in the bud. Stand up for yourself like you would for a child who is being bullied. This is your life, and you have the right to be here.

Remember that you are just as worthy and deserving of love, happiness, and success as anyone else. With that right comes the power to make choices and shape your life as you wish.

Remember Jenny? She had great difficulty with this and couldn't look at herself in the mirror at the beginning of our sessions. She revealed that she hadn't looked at herself in the mirror for years. By working on subtle shifts in her perception and breaking down her negative self-talk, she quickly saw the beauty within reflected in the mirror.

And even Jane Fonda, who in all regards is a beautiful person. Do you think she would have resorted to having plastic surgery if she were more accepting of her body and her right to exist? I think not.

When working on this level of self-confidence, we must investigate what your Solar Plexus is doing.

Confidence Begins Within the Solar Plexus

The Solar Plexus Chakra, also known as Manipura, is the third Chakra in the human body. Represented by the color yellow, it is located in the solar plexus, just above the navel. It represents your ego identity, self-definition, and the realization of separateness and autonomy. It is your power center. Think of what happens when two men are arguing; they puff up their chests. See Figure 6.

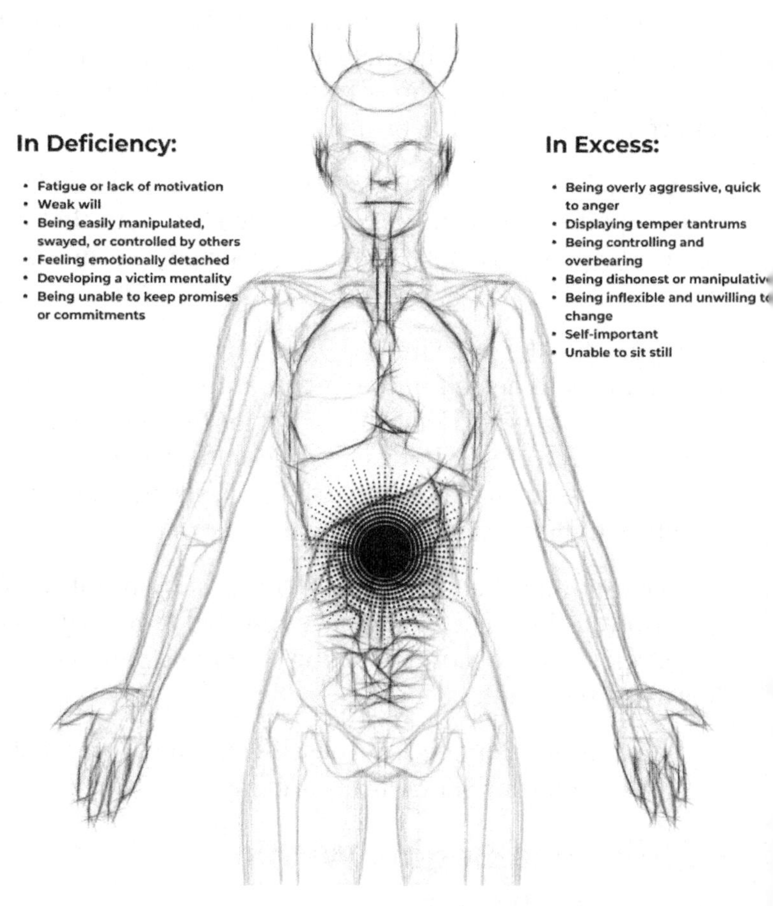

Figure 6. Solar Plexus Chakra

When this power center is balanced, you exhibit positive traits and characteristics. You are responsible and self-disciplined, taking ownership of your actions and decisions. You are reliable, dependable, and trustworthy. Additional benefits include feeling good about yourself and having high self-esteem. You project a warm, approachable, and perhaps even playful attitude. You are more spontaneous and open to new experiences because you are sure of your ability to meet and overcome possible challenges. Overall, you feel secure in yourself, your presence, and your abilities.

But like all other chakras, the balance can be upset. Several events or experiences can lead to an imbalance in the solar plexus chakra. Being made to feel ashamed or embarrassed is one. So too, is constantly feeling controlled or dominated by others.

Feelings of helplessness can manifest when forced to do things against your will, whether being physically abused or living in a constant state of fear of punishment. All of these states lead to feelings of inadequacy and low self-esteem. Such situations make it difficult to tap into your power.

When the solar plexus chakra is in a state of deficiency, the physical and emotional symptoms include:

- Low energy that manifests in feelings of fatigue or lack of motivation
- Weak will, which leads to having difficulty making decisions or sticking to them
- Being easily manipulated, swayed, or controlled by others
- Feeling emotionally detached
- Having a low body temperature

- Experiencing stomach problems or difficulty digesting food
- Relying on external stimulants like caffeine or sugar to boost energy
- Developing a victim mentality
- Being unable to keep promises or commitments

When the solar plexus chakra is overactive or in excess, physical behavior includes:

- Being overly aggressive, quick to anger, and easily provoked
- Displaying temper tantrums
- Being controlling and overbearing in relationships
- Always needing to have the last word or win arguments
- Being dishonest or manipulative
- Being inflexible and unwilling to change
- Having an inflated sense of self-importance
- Having excessive energy or being unable to sit still

And like the other chakras, you can bring the solar plexus chakra back into balance with conscious mind-body practices such as meditation and visualization techniques.

Solar Plexus Chakra visualization

Sit in a comfortable position and close your eyes. Visualize a bright yellow light shining just below the ribs at your diaphragm. As you breathe in, imagine this light growing brighter; as you breathe out, imagine any negative energy or tension leaving your body. Repeat this visualization for several minutes or as long as you feel comfortable.

Practice the Mantra RAM

It is simple to practice. Sit comfortably. Close your eyes. Repeat the mantra "Ram" or "I am" silently to yourself. This mantra is associated with bringing balance and mental clarity.

Affirmations

Another technique to adjust the mind and balance this Chakra is with these affirmations:

- "I am strong and confident."
- "I trust in my power."
- "I am worthy of love and respect."
- "I am capable of achieving my goals."
- "I attract abundance and success."
- "I am in charge of my destiny."
- "I am filled with self-love and self-acceptance."
- "I radiate positive energy and confidence."

Crystalline Energy and Aromatherapy

Certain crystals (such as Citrine, Tiger's Eye, and Yellow Jasper) and practicing aromatherapy with essential oils like peppermint, lemon, and ginger helps balance the solar plexus chakra.

Claim Your Right to be Here

In one of my favorite TED talks [27], Amy Cuddy explains that our body language is not just a reflection of our emotions but also shapes our emotions and affects our hormone levels. She researched posture and found that when we adopt power poses, such as standing tall with our chest open and our arms raised, the act increases testosterone levels, a hormone associated with confidence and assertiveness, and decreases the levels of the stress hormone cortisol. On the other hand, when we adopt low-power poses, such as slouching with our arms crossed, it has the opposite effect, increasing cortisol levels and decreasing testosterone.

Cuddy also argues that these physiological changes affect how we feel and how we present ourselves. When we adopt a power pose, our behavior and communication show confidence. Conversely, when we adopt a low power pose, we feel more anxious and submissive, and this, too, shows in our interactions with other people.

Her research suggests that by being aware of our posture and actively choosing to adopt power poses, we can improve our confidence and reduce stress in our daily lives.

A few power poses that you can adopt into your daily routine (along with instructions to do them) include:

The Wonder Woman

Stand with your feet hip-width apart, your hands on your hips, and your chest open.

The Victory

Stand with your feet hip-width apart. Lift your arms over your head. Interlock your fingers.

The Superhero

Standing with your feet hip-width apart, place your hands on your hips and push your chest out.

The Expansive

Sit with your legs spread apart and your arms resting behind your head.

The Alpha

Sit with your feet on the floor. Lean forward with your hands clasped together and your elbows on your knees.

It's worth noting that the hormone changes induced by power poses are temporary. They usually last for around 20 minutes after the posture is adopted. However, the effect becomes long-lasting if these power poses are adopted consistently.

Power poses are not a magic solution and may not be appropriate in all situations, such as in a formal or conservative setting. But when used intentionally and consistently and in conjunction with other strategies for managing stress and building self-esteem, power poses can be a helpful tool for improving confidence and reducing stress. Check in with yourself throughout the day and adjust your posture to project that outward calm and poise.

Cultivate Body Confidence

Your body is a sacred and divine temple, as it is the vessel that houses your mind and heart. As such, it is only fitting that your body is treated with respect and reverence. This view of worship toward your body is one that I invite you to adopt.

By thinking of your body as a divine temple, you shift your focus from its external appearance to its internal functions and abilities. Instead of criticizing and judging yourself, learn to appreciate your body's unique and impressive capabilities, such as its ability to heal, move, think, feel, and create. Additionally, by seeing your body as revered, you will be more inclined to make healthy choices such as eating nutritious food, getting enough sleep, and being physically active.

Practicing healthier ways of thinking about yourself and your body is essential in building body confidence.

Other things you can do include:

Keep a top-ten list of things you like about yourself.

Write down what you are grateful for about your body and what it allows you to do, like walking, running, dancing, and playing with your kids.

Remind yourself that "true beauty" is not simply skin-deep.

True beauty encompasses a person's character, values, and overall well-being. It is not limited to physical appearance.

Look at yourself as a whole person.

Recognize that your body is only one aspect of who you are. You are a complex and multi-faceted person with unique qualities, abilities, and interests.

Surround yourself with positive people.

Spend time with people who make you feel good about yourself, lift you, and encourage you to be your best self.

Shut down the negative voices in your head.

When you notice yourself having negative thoughts about your body, take a step back and question the validity of those thoughts. Are they based on facts, or are they just negative assumptions? They may even be words someone else has said that you have taken up the habit of repeating about your body. Replace negative thoughts with positive affirmations.

Wear comfortable clothes that fit your body now.

Your body is unique. It's important to dress it in a way that acknowledges that uniqueness and makes you feel good. Steps for doing so include:

- Get measured so you can choose clothes that fit your body now.
- Shop for your current size. Don't buy clothes that are too small or too big with the hope that you will fit into them eventually.
- Choose clothes made of comfortable and breathable fabrics.

- Experiment with different styles to find what works for you.
- Embrace your body shape and choose clothes that flatter your figure.
- Wear clothes that you feel comfortable and confident in, regardless of fashion trends or societal expectations.

Become a critical viewer of social media messages.

Be mindful of the media you consume. Surround yourself with content that uplifts you, inspires you, and makes you feel good about yourself.

Do something nice for yourself.

Taking care of yourself is not a luxury. It is a necessity, just like all other needs. Treat yourself to a spa day. Plan a day trip. Escape on a weekend getaway. Take a class or workshop. Do something nice for yourself today to improve your self-esteem.

Help others.

Everyone's journey with body confidence is unique. Just as you might struggle with improving yours, so too do others. Help others when you can by being patient, kind, and supportive. Helping others improve their perception of their body can positively impact their lives and help create a more body-positive culture. It's as simple as complimenting someone every day. And it just feels good.

Fill the Space You're in

When you care for your body and "Clean Your House," you clean your mind and shift your energy. You will fill your space with positive energy and project confidence and self-assurance. You show the world that by accepting yourself with loving kindness, you also accept others. It makes you more approachable and attractive and helps you stand out in situations where you want to be noticed, such as job interviews, public speaking, or social events. By projecting high energy, you show the world that you have claimed your distinct right to be in that space and that you are worthy of attention.

Your energy might not be as high as you want it to be, but with mindful, intentional effort, you will elevate your vibration with these practices. And when you start shifting out of the lower vibration energy and aligning with your desired state of being, you are practicing self-love.

Next up on your journey: We'll add on clear intentions, continue to focus on the positive, and take action that will move you closer to your best life.

STEP #3

Create Your Happy Life (Self-Confidence)

Because one believes in oneself,
one doesn't try to convince.
Because one is content with oneself,
one doesn't need others' approval.
Because one accepts oneself,
the whole world accepts him or her.
Lao Tzu

CHAPTER 7

Speak with Confidence

When I was in clinical practice as a Holistic Nutritionist, 90% of my clients (mostly women) were diagnosed with hyperthyroidism and were on medication. Upon further investigation, besides the high levels of stress in their lives, I discovered that these clients struggled with speaking up for themselves.

Curious, I searched for and found a study conducted with women between the ages of 20-89 in the United States that confirmed my findings. The results indicated that women were 5-10 times more likely to experience thyroid dysfunction than men.[28] Why do you think that is?

Remember our discussion in Chapter 4 about the "Not Good Enough Culture?" We are constantly struggling to find our place and our voice. We don't want to seem pushy because we prefer to collaborate, but when we aren't in a culture of collaboration but competition, then we struggle to find our voice and either get shut down or opt to shut down ourselves—further adding to our lack of self-confidence and creating an enormous amount of stress.

Hyperthyroidism and stress have a complex relationship. Stress can cause an increase in the levels of hormones such as cortisol and adrenaline. They mimic the symptoms of hyperthyroidism. However, hyperthyroidism can also cause stress due to the symptoms it causes. Also, individuals with hyperthyroidism tend to have a higher susceptibility to stress as the condition disrupts the normal functioning of the hypothalamic-pituitary-adrenal (HPA) axis. It's a bit of a "Catch-22" with the delicate thyroid gland.

Let's dig further. The thyroid is a gland positioned in the neck. One of its functions is to produce hormones that regulate metabolism and energy levels. The most common hormones, called thyroxine (T4) and triiodothyronine (T3), help maintain normal growth and development as well as overall health.

Stress either has a positive or a negative effect on the thyroid gland. The acute stress of a one-time event causes a temporary increase in thyroid hormone production. This increases the body's metabolism and energy levels as part of the normal stress response. But chronic stress, on the other hand, hurts the thyroid gland. Prolonged exposure to stress increases levels of cortisol. Cortisol suppresses the regular utility of the thyroid and leads to an underactive thyroid - hypothyroidism. The symptoms of hypothyroidism are plentiful, including fatigue, weight gain, and depression. Chronic stress can also lead to an overactive thyroid - hyperthyroidism. Symptoms of the latter include mood swings, sensitivity to heat, nervousness, anxiety, and irritability.

Shutting yourself down and not saying what you need to (in an appropriate way) causes stress that results in health issues. Yes, it does.

And science [29] proves it. The impact of stress on a person's health is multifaceted, varying from person to person.

Factors such as genetics, coping strategies, personality type, and social support all play a role in determining an individual's susceptibility to thyroid problems due to stress.

When you become grounded, self-aware, and self-accepting, as I hope you have by now, your interpretation of stress will change. And you'll start trusting your intuition which will lead to more self-confidence and an ability to speak your truth.

Trust Your Intuition to Speak

Intuition is the brain's ability to quickly draw on past experiences and external cues to make decisions at an unconscious level. You may also use the phrase "gut intuition." Appropriately named as neurotransmitters present in the gut respond to environmental stimuli and emotions and send signals to the brain to help with decision-making.

Women are inherently more in tune with their intuition compared to men. This is why the term "women's intuition" was created. This difference is the product of evolution as it has helped females better understand and predict the needs of their offspring and mates. It also made us better protectors to keep the people we love safe from potential threats.

Women's intuition is often begging us to stand up for ourselves when so often, our power is being stripped away by various circumstances. When that something in our stomachs says to speak up for ourselves, we often don't heed its direction and let things slide even when we know we shouldn't. Difficulty speaking up for ourselves stems from a lack of self-confidence, a fear of rejection or conflict, or past experiences that have led to feelings of powerlessness.

On a metaphysical level, this inability to speak your truth indicates that your throat chakra is blocked or malfunctioning. See Figure 7.

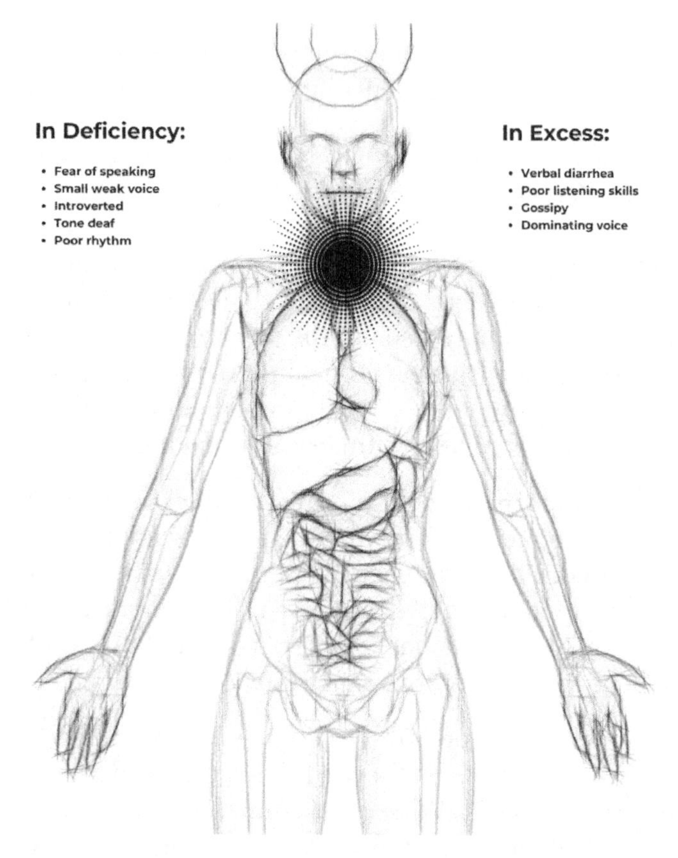

Figure 7. The Throat Chakra

Express through the Throat Chakra

The throat chakra is also called Vishuddha in Sanskrit. It is the fifth chakra in the body and, as the title suggests, is located in the throat. Blue activates this chakra, representing communication, creativity, listening, resonance, finding one's voice, and sense of hearing.

When your throat chakra is balanced, you communicate effectively and authentically and express yourself freely in a manner only derived from having a sense of inner truth and integrity. You speak your truth without reservation because you recognize it is your right to do so. As an effective communicator, you realize it is not all about you. Communication is a two-way street, so you actively listen to and empathize with others.

The timing and rhythm of your speech and actions have great flow because instinct guides you to know when to speak and when to remain silent. You may also be in tune with your creative side and express yourself through art forms such as writing, music, and singing.

When the throat chakra is blocked or imbalanced, the difference is like night and day. The words seem locked within, and when they do come out, they tend to be in a weak or aggressive voice. You have difficulty communicating, feel unsure of how to express yourself, and feel incapable of speaking your truth.

A weak voice or fear of speaking indicates a deficient throat chakra. When in excess, the throat chakra can be overactive, and you can exhibit symptoms like verbal diarrhea, poor listening skills, gossiping, and the frequent use of a dominating voice. Physical symptoms like disorders of the throat, ears, voice, neck, and mouth, thyroid malfunctioning, immune system breakdown, and metabolic syndrome are common.

Events that upset the balance of the throat chakra include being verbally abused, receiving excessive criticism, being subjected to authoritarian parenting, and having a family history of alcohol or drug dependency.

In detail, verbal abuse from a partner, family member, or authority figure leads to feelings of powerlessness and a fear of speaking out. Excessive criticism, whether it's from others or one's self, can lead to feelings of self-doubt and stubs one's ability to express themselves. Authoritarian parenting, where children are not allowed to express themselves or speak up, often leads to adults who have difficulty communicating effectively and expressing themselves freely. A family history of alcohol or chemical dependency can negatively impact the balance of the throat chakra because a lack of trust develops when the consequences are unpredictable. If this information is triggering, please go back to your forgiveness practices.

Let's focus on practices to activate and balance the throat chakra.

Practice the Mantra HAM

Sit comfortably or standing. Close your eyes and focus on the throat. Repeat the mantra "Ham" silently or loudly to yourself. Envision the throat opening up with the feeling of the vibration. Combine the visualization of blue light in the throat with this mantra. And wear a turquoise necklace.

Affirmations

Speak affirmations that activate your confident voice, such as:

- "I hear and speak the truth."
- "I express myself with clear intent."
- "Creativity flows in and through me."

Include any chanting, singing, or storytelling.

Silence is also a powerful tool for unblocking the throat chakra. It brings you in touch with your inner voice to better connect with your truth. This connection allows for better communication when you do have to speak.

There are infinite ways to be silent with intention so that you hear what is going on within more clearly. You can sit still and let silence engulf you as you reflect. You can also journal or go for nature walks.

When We don't Say What We Mean

I have a pet peeve, and it's Passive-Aggressive communication. Passive-aggressive communication is a type of communication in which a person expresses negative feelings, resentment, or aggression indirectly or subtly rather than directly expressing their thoughts or feelings.

Examples of passive-aggressive communication include:

- Using sarcasm
- Giving backhanded compliments
- Blame and criticizing
- Making statements such as "I'm fine" when you are not
- Withholding information by not responding to messages or avoiding communication
- Not following through on commitments or agreements
- Agreeing to something instead of expressing your true desire, which may be contrary

Passive-aggressive behavior can develop as a response to resentment and opposition to the demands of others, particularly those in positions of authority. People who use passive-aggressive communication may feel that they are not being heard or that their needs are not being met. As such, they use this type of communication to express their frustration and resistance while avoiding confrontation.

Passive-aggressive behavior can also manifest as resistance to cooperation, procrastination, and intentional mistakes in response to others' demands. It may be the only way this person thinks they can assert autonomy and resist being controlled or manipulated by others.

A cynical, sullen, or hostile attitude and frequent complaints about feeling underappreciated or cheated are common traits associated with passive-aggressive behavior. Unfortunately, this behavior is not always easy to recognize, especially in oneself. It is not always intentional but learned as a survival mechanism because expressing true thoughts and feelings has often led to dealing with turbulent circumstances.

The Remedy for Passive Aggression

You do not clearly convey your wants and needs when you use passive-aggressive communication. Instead, it only leads you down a road of misunderstandings and conflicts. It makes it difficult for others to understand your perspective, so feelings of being unloved or disrespected arise.

Passive-aggressive communication creates a vicious cycle of unmet needs, resentments, and frustration. The person on the receiving end may feel confused, frustrated, or resentful because they don't understand the underlying message. This leads to a lack of trust, poor communication, and dissatisfaction in relationships. It also contributes to feelings of isolation and low self-esteem.

But there is a solution for unlocking the strength of your voice.

1. Be brave

Be authentic. Be transparent with your emotions and intentions, making communication clear and direct. There is no other way. Effective communication is not always accessible because it requires vulnerability but leads to deeper connections and understanding with others.

2. Be an emotional unit when communicating

Create a safe space for open and honest communication. It is not a battle. All parties want to feel heard and validated. As such, there needs to be a willingness to compromise and take responsibility for your emotions.

3. Be specific – no innuendos

State your thoughts and feelings directly without hiding behind hints or implications. Innuendos increase the likelihood of you being misunderstood. But when you are specific with your requests, it will prevent misunderstandings and create trust.

4. Don't blame

Blaming others creates an atmosphere of defensiveness and makes it difficult for the other person to hear what you are saying. Instead of casting blame, use "I" statements to express your feelings rather than making accusations. For example, instead of saying, "You always make me feel this way," say, "I feel this way when this happens."

5. Don't apologize for your needs

Your needs are valid, and authentically expressing them is a must to ensure your happiness in any relationship. Trust and intimacy are built into relationships when you and other people do this mutually.

When communicating, keep these two rules of thumb in mind:

1. **If you feel anxious** – like you're on the verge of acting out or falling back on past coping mechanisms - stop, take a deep breath, and ask yourself, "What are my needs?" Develop this answer in your head first. Then deliver it to the other person calmly.
2. **If you feel avoidant** – like you're ready to bolt – ask for the space you need to recollect your thoughts. Be respectful of the other person's feelings as you do this.

Remember that you have the right to speak up and express your thoughts regardless of the situation. Become confident in your ability to convey your needs without fear of reprimand.

CHAPTER 8

Protect Your Boundaries

Setting boundaries, particularly for women, is a complex and challenging issue due to societal and cultural expectations and norms. History shows that women who asserted their autonomy or denied men perceived privileges were ostracized, discriminated against, and punished with violence. The reality is that not much has changed with the treatment of women and boundaries.

The treatment of women as second-class citizens and the suppression of their rights and freedoms still exist in many parts of the world, including the supposed FREE WORLD of western culture. We've seen this in North America over the past 30 years with abortion rights laws. The idea that men could make laws restricting women from caring for their bodies seems ludicrous to me. Fundamental rights for women mean even less in countries run by religious extremists.

Take, for example; the attention brought to the treatment of women in Iran in recent times. The Iranian legal system is based on a distorted extreme version of Islamic law. Women in Iran face discrimination in many areas, including marriage, divorce, inheritance, and child custody. They are also underrepresented in political and economic leadership positions. The same is true in other parts of the world that stay true to extreme religions.

The truth is women have always had to fight for the rights that men are given freely. Beyond rights and freedoms, women in the Western world are also not exempt from having their boundaries disrespected. The Weinstein and Epstein cases were high-profile incidents of sexual misconduct and abuse that came to light in the early 2010s and continue today. These high-profile cases highlight the injustices women face in a part of the world where freedom has been supposedly deemed for all.

The Weinstein and Epstein cases, among others, have brought to light the issue of women being complicit in keeping secret the bad behavior of men. Many individuals, including other women, were aware of the misconduct in these cases but chose not to speak out or take action. They kept silent for various reasons, including fear of retaliation, a lack of belief that their voices would be heard, or a belief that it was not their place to speak out.

It highlights the convoluted dynamics of power and manipulation that occur in situations of sexual misconduct and abuse and how societal norms and expectations contribute to the silencing of victims and witnesses. It also shows the importance of creating a culture and environment where individuals feel safe and encouraged to speak out and where there are clear and effective channels for reporting and addressing such behavior.

The lack of respect for boundaries that protect women is also in the boardroom.[30] Sexual harassment is a widespread issue in the workplace, disproportionately affecting women: One *of every two women will be harassed at some point during their academic or working lives.* One reason for this is that many victims stay silent about their experiences due to fear of consequences or a lack of belief that speaking up will make a difference. When women do try to speak up, they face three main barriers:

1. They are required to prove that their experience is significant.
2. They are expected to trust the system (which traditionally shows much bias) to handle their complaints.
3. They may face severe consequences, such as damage to their reputation for challenging the system.

This is the reality in which we live. So how do you use the tools of boundaries to mitigate any of these situations? You become an expert at creating boundaries so that it is apparent to those around you that you are not a candidate for harassment or abuse in any regard.

Setting Boundaries Often Goes Against Women's Primal Needs

Boundaries are the guidelines that tell other people our values, beliefs, and expectations in our interactions and relationships with them. Boundaries fall into different categories. They can be physical, emotional, mental, and spiritual and include personal space, time, privacy, emotions, beliefs, and limits on what types of behavior or communication we accept or do not in a given relationship.

Boundaries are not limited to any one area in life. They hold true for various areas like friendships, romantic relationships, family ties, and professional relationships. In a personal relationship, boundaries may include how much time is spent together, how communication is handled, and how disagreements are settled. In a work setting, boundaries may consist of guidelines around working hours, communication with colleagues, and handling of confidential information.

Setting personal boundaries is an essential aspect of self-care and self-protection. Having clear boundaries also helps maintain healthy relationships through communicating individual needs and wants and respecting the boundaries of both parties. It also reduces stress and anxiety by allowing us to control our time and energy.

Setting personal boundaries is a complex process for women as it is tied to their primal needs for safety and security for themselves and their families. Many women have internalized messages that they are not worthy of setting boundaries or that their needs are not as important as others. As such, it is not just a matter of learning to assert oneself but also addressing underlying feelings and emotions and shifting our energy to align with our boundaries.

Where they end and you begin

Setting boundaries in a culture that promotes having no boundaries, as we see on social media, can be challenging. We have to expose everything we do, from what we eat, to how we dress and what we believe in, on a minute-by-minute basis. And if we forget to document every detail, then we lose popularity.

The result of having no boundaries on social media is depression and anxiety. A study [31] *revealed that more time spent using social media was significantly associated with greater symptoms of dispositional anxiety.*

In relationships, having no boundaries can manifest as codependent behavior. The need to overlap your wants and desires with your partner's and the belief that your happiness depends on theirs dominates your sense of self. You might have caught yourself saying," I can't be happy if my partner isn't," Or "Happy wife, happy life." And "You don't marry someone you can live with — you marry someone you cannot live without."

Are any of these true? You really can't live or be happy without someone in your life? If you said yes to this question, then I want to remind you of what the Dalai Lama says,

"Spend some time alone every day."

Taking time to know what you want and do not want in your life is the foundation of building a better, happier life. When you put yourself last on your list of important people, you tell the world that you do not deserve to be first.

Imagine your energy is a bucket of water. If you constantly give your energy without replenishing it, you will be empty and have nothing to offer. Remember, you train people in your life how to treat you. If you're constantly giving without receiving, you might become resentful and fall into the pattern of being a victim. And this is what we are trying to avoid in this journey of self-love.

You can create solid boundaries and live with an open heart. With loving awareness as your guide, establishing boundaries in a kind but firm way shows that you respect yourself and the people around you.

In a Psychology Today [31] article by Lisa A. Phillips called "The Endless Love," Lisa highlights the problem with ambiguity during breakups and reveals that collaborating on an Exit Plan with your partner can mitigate heartbreak. I love this idea because it shows respect for you and your partner during a highly charged emotional event.

Clear boundaries allow you to establish your physical and emotional limits. Boundaries help you stay grounded and calm. You become confident and no longer allow others to infiltrate your energetic field. This goes hand-in-hand with re-establishing your integrity.

Back to Meredith

Meredith struggled with setting boundaries with her ex-husband. Even when she sensed that he was manipulating her, she couldn't break the emotional bond that kept her connected to him and his demands. Meredith returned to him multiple times despite knowing that it was wrong. It was a mystery to her why she couldn't detach herself from this unhealthy relationship.

It's a great example of how powerful our emotional connections with other people can be. We've all likely experienced instances where we think of someone, and then they reach out to us unexpectedly - a testament to the power of our thoughts and energy.

We are all energy beings, and while we interact with the world through our physical senses, our primary means of relating is through energy. In relationships, we develop energetic connections or bonds. These links are not necessarily negative; they help us form important alliances with others.

Energetic bonds (also called soul contracts) aren't exclusive to romantic relationships. They can also exist in relationships with family members, employers, and friends. It is essential to evaluate relationships that drain more energy than they give regularly.

Identify relationships that don't make you feel good and examine why you cannot sever ties with that person. A story or belief often keeps you connected to those individuals.

Meredith felt guilty about setting boundaries with her ex-partner because she felt like a "bad" person for separating from him when he had cancer. It was curious to her how quickly he recovered. She finally found the courage to distance herself. And his manipulative tactics became apparent. Infuriated that he couldn't control her any longer, he stalked her and left messages accusing her of being cruel for leaving him after everything they had been through.

She took another courageous step, blocked him on all her devices, and finally reported him to the police. Finally, he released her from the energetic soul contract allowing her to heal.

Once you have established a boundary, the next phase of creating healthy boundaries is done on an energetic level.

Create Boundaries on An Energetic Level

Breaking a soul contract is difficult when you're in a toxic relationship. You feel unable to release its hold on you. However, understanding the underlying story and energy behind the relationship helps you finally break free, as we did with Meredith.

Energy plays a significant role in our relationships and how we interact with others. As energetic beings, our thoughts and emotions create thought forms that attach to others, otherwise known as energetic cording. If you are intuitive and energetically sensitive, you may be more aware of how other people's energy can impact you. For example, you may feel collective fear in a group or feel a sense of love and joy during a live performance.

When it's time to release these bonds, we look to removing energetic cords by breaking soul contracts as an effective practice in energy work. Breaking a soul contract is not limited to past relationships or even those that drain us. You can also practice this to maintain a clean energy flow and create space for new connections with other people.

Energy cords are like tubes connecting us to another person, with energy flowing back and forth. If the connection drains us, the energy will flow away from us. If it nourishes us, the energy will flow toward us.

When we hold on to relationships for too long or give energy when we don't have enough to provide leads to an imbalance, where we feel depleted and anxious around that person. If a relationship ends and you still feel depleted or anxious at the thought of them, this means that your cord has not been severed completely.

Signs of unhealthy cording include:

- depletion of energy
- feelings of being stuck or unable to make decisions
- obsessive thoughts
- lowered immune function
- and unhealthy habits

As we grow and evolve, we must let go of what no longer serves us to create space for potential and possibility. This process is essential for growth and personal development. However, when emotional contracts bind us on a soul level, the cord may be thick and strong, making the process more complicated.

Soul contracts occur from ancient programs passed down from our parents and ancestors. They can skew our ability to function in the world. Their binds restrict our choices. These contracts can lead to addiction, codependency, and other toxic patterns that repress our life force and prevent us from being happy and fulfilled.

While there may be valuable lessons in these soul attachments, it's not necessary to remain connected to people when the association becomes harmful. Break free from soul contracts when they disrupt rather than elevate your life. The nature of the relationship is irrelevant. Whether it's a romantic partner, co-worker, or family member, if a relationship is destructive and stressful, the unspoken bond or familiarity that keeps you unhealthily attached to this person can easily be broken.

Breaking a Soul Contract

1. Identify the type of relationship you have with the person. Search deep in your soul and formulate a clear, articulate answer. For example, you may say to yourself, "I am in a romantic relationship."
2. Identify what it feels like to be in that relationship. For example, "I feel suffocated in this relationship" or "I feel conditions in this relationship."
3. Ascertain the type of contract you have with this person. For example, "I feel like I'm responsible for their happiness. Therefore, I sacrifice my own for their comfort."

4. Decide the intensity of this contract by picking a material to represent its weight in your life. Examples of materials include paper, leather, steel, and stone.
5. Finally, use a tool like scissors, a knife, or a hammer to destroy the contract entirely.

While we are all interconnected, when you understand how to break a soul contract through your energetic power, you grant yourself the liberty to move forward peacefully.

The "FUCK NO" Method

When you clearly understand what brings you happiness and a sense of grounding, setting boundaries comes naturally. However, if you're still unsure when your boundaries have been crossed due to past experiences, using the "FUCK NO" method is helpful.

This method helps you make decisions about where your boundaries are. The more you use it, the easier it becomes to identify them.

Ask yourself the following questions when confronted by a problematic interaction:

- Does this feel right in my body?
- Is this for the good of my life and soul?
- Will this diminish me or force me to sacrifice my integrity?

If the answer to any of these questions is "no," "I'm not sure," or "maybe," then it's a "FUCK NO." There are no grey areas.

Saying "NO" can be difficult when you don't have much practice doing it, especially when you are hard-wired as a caregiver like Meredith was. However, drawing that line is a necessary part of self-protection and self-preservation.

Here are some practical ways to say no in different situations:

- "I appreciate the offer, but I won't be able to participate."
- "I'm not interested in that now, but you should go for it."
- "I'm not feeling up to it right now. Maybe another time."
- "I need to think about it more before I can answer."
- "It's hard to say no, but I must put my well-being first."
- "I'm not available for that right now, but thank you for considering me."
- "I need to build more trust before I can commit to that."
- "No. Thank you for understanding."
- "I'm unable to commit to that today."
- "I'm sorry, but that's not something I can do at this time."
- "I value our connection, but that request doesn't align with my values."

Develop your own phrases that feel authentic to you and that you are comfortable using. Pick two of these as your go-to phrases when setting a boundary. By using these phrases, you assert your boundaries politely and respectfully. With practice, you'll be able to find the right words in any situation.

CHAPTER 9

Create Happiness Every Single Day

Years ago, while searching for my happiness, I met a Clinical Psychologist from Berlin who believed that the North American way of optimism was unrealistic and hedonistic. Defensively, I exclaimed that having a positive outlook on life was vital to finding purpose and making my journey to self-love more tolerable. I held on to my often-contrived sense of happiness to cope. "What's the point if I'm not happy?" I would say to myself. Years later, I understood what he was trying to say.

The concept of self-love has been viewed in different ways throughout history. Hinduism and Jainism view self-love as a major sin that ultimately leads to harm. Confucianism values society over the self. Aristotle argued that people who love themselves to achieve unwarranted personal gain are bad, but those who love themselves to achieve virtuous principles are the best sort of good. Jesus prioritized the love of God and commanded the love of other people as one's self. In Christianity, early followers such as Paul the Apostle and James believed that inordinate self-love opposed the love of God. However, American Historian of Religions Elaine Pagels argues that Jesus taught that self-love was intrinsic to neighborly or brotherly love. And Christian monk Evagrius Ponticus believed excessive self-love was one of eight key sins.

Not every traditional view of self-love is opposed. Buddhism taught that the desires of the self are the root of all evil. However, this is balanced with Karuna (compassion), the ability to empathize with others and to feel concerned for them. It is one of the four immeasurables in Buddhism, along with loving-kindness, equanimity, and sympathetic joy. Karuna is an essential aspect of spiritual development as it allows for understanding and alleviating the suffering of others. In this way, it is a powerful antidote to the ego-driven desires that lead to suffering and unhappiness.

In modern times, self-love has become essential to mental and emotional well-being. Mental health professionals and self-help gurus, myself included, emphasize the importance of self-love to overcome negative thoughts, depression, and anxiety. To take care of others, we must first learn to take care of ourselves. Self-compassion and self-care are not selfish or vain. Instead, they are necessary for achieving balance, inner peace, and meaningful connection with others.

Come Back to Yourself

Finding your internal happiness comes with a price. Similar to the stories we dismantled to rebuild our sense of self-love, there must be hell before we get to heaven. It's the only way.

Self-love is a journey that leads you back to yourself. It takes you back to the part of you that got left behind when you started putting others ahead of yourself. By focusing on filling your bucket first, you'll be able to share in the wealth of self-worth and confidence.

The heart needs nurturing to open.

We've tapped into the power of The Heart, Throat, Solar Plexus, and Root Chakras along our journey. And the human body contains seven centers of chakra energy. Each chakra has a vital function and corresponds to a particular area of the endocrine body which governs specific physical and emotional processes. But the heart chakra is located at the center of it all. When it is open and its energy flows freely, a person can give and receive love abundantly and easily.

The heart chakra is the bridge between the lower chakras, associated with physical and material needs, and the upper chakras, associated with spiritual connection and awareness. The heart chakra balances and integrates the energy of the lower and upper chakras. As such, when it is open and balanced, a person can easily access both the physical and spiritual realms.

The heart chakra is the first responder of sorts because it senses and responds to emotional and energetic changes before the brain and mind are aware of them. This is because the heart chakra is connected to the body's energetic system, which is more sensitive and responsive than the physical nervous system. Heart energy is intuitive; it senses when something isn't right or when things are going well before we even have time to process it mentally.

Tap into this higher level of consciousness by living through your heart. Living in a heart-centered way means making decisions and taking actions guided by love, compassion, and empathy. Once you've cleared your energy to receive all the goodness of your desires, the final step is manifesting the life you've always wanted. To do this, you must develop habits that keep you focused on your goals.

Become a Happiness High Performer

High performers and successful individuals often have a strong sense of self-worth and self-confidence to help them achieve their goals and overcome obstacles. However, even successful people can struggle with self-doubt and insecurities. In Jane Fonda's interview, she stated, "I have to work every day to be self-accepting; it doesn't come easy to me."

Building self-confidence and self-worth require consistent effort, just like physical training. It involves setting and achieving small goals, practicing self-compassion, learning to accept and embrace imperfections, and working on positive self-talk. It's also important to understand that success doesn't have one single definition. It is a personal and subjective concept; it is different for everyone.

What does success mean for you? For some, success is defined by professional accomplishments like reaching a high-level position in their career or earning a certain level of income. Success may be determined by personal relationships like having a happy and healthy family or fulfilling and loving relationships. For others, success may be defined by personal growth and self-improvement, such as becoming more self-aware, confident, or content. For most, it is a combination of indicators, as achieving success in one area of life does not guarantee that a person will have high self-worth and self-confidence. Take time to reflect and define what success means for you because it will help you set goals and make decisions that align with your values, priorities, and authentic self.

Brendan Burchard is the author of the bestselling book *High Performance Habits: How Extraordinary People Become That Way*. According to the lessons taught in *this book*, there are seven fundamental characteristics of high performers:

1. **High performance is not a result of inherent talent or a specific personality type but rather a combination of good habits and increased confidence.**

Brendan conducted one of the most extensive studies on high performance and found that factors such as gender, race, age, and personality traits have little impact. Instead, consistent practice and other habits set high performers apart.

Additionally, high performers possess a strong belief in their ability to master even complex tasks. This is not an inherent trait but rather an earned confidence achieved through diligent practice.

2. **High performers possess a strong sense of self-awareness and have a clear understanding of their purpose in life.**

They consistently reflect on the big questions, such as how they want to be remembered and what they want to accomplish in life. This habit is referred to as *seeking clarity*, and it helps them to maintain a clear focus on their goals and priorities. This habit is not limited to specific times of the year like birthdays or New Year's Eve, but it's a constant reflection and self-discovery process. It keeps them goal-oriented and motivated.

3. **High performers are known for their positive outlook on life and their commitment to maintaining both physical and mental fitness.**

They prioritize their physical health by exercising regularly and maintaining a healthy diet. They also make an effort to maintain mental fitness through practices such as meditation and mindfulness. This allows them to have energy levels similar to those of professional athletes, which is a key habit for maintaining a high-performance level. Additionally, successful CEOs often have effective scheduling habits and the ability to stay focused and minimize distractions.

4. **High performers stay motivated by using both inner and outer expectations.**

They set both personal and external goals and use them to push themselves to achieve more. An example of this is of two runners about to start a race. Both have similar track records and have put in the same amount of training. The runner who has a personal goal, such as winning for the sake of glory, may perform well. But the runner who has an external motivation, such as winning for their mother, will likely perform better as they have an added level of stimulus.

5. **High performers are effective at avoiding distractions and managing their time efficiently.**

They prioritize important tasks and work on them first rather than getting bogged down by unimportant ones. This increases their productivity as they get more done in less time. They are also smart with deadlines and know how to set realistic timeframes for completing tasks to prevent feeling overwhelmed and stressed.

6. **High performers possess the ability to build strong and meaningful relationships with their peers.**

They don't fall into the "lonely at the top" mentality. Instead, they are appreciative, giving, and aware of what others need to succeed. They understand the importance of building a support system and surrounding themselves with people who will help them achieve their goals. This characteristic serves them in both their personal and professional lives.

7. **High performers are openly ambitious and are not afraid to take risks.**

They are willing to step out of their comfort zones and take on new challenges. Additionally, they have a positive perspective on challenging situations, which allows them to approach risks with a mindset of growth and learning rather than fear of failure.

It's okay if you still need to possess these characteristics, as they can be learned and developed through practice and effort.

Happy Every Day Method

If you applied these traits to your life areas (health and fitness, intellectual, emotional, spiritual, relationships, financial, career, quality of life, and life vision), how would each area look?

Let's do a little exercise. If you gave each life area a happiness score out of 10, with ten being completely fulfilled, what would each area score? If you feel anything less than completely fulfilled in any area, this indicates a need for improvement.

Remember, you are on the path to growth. There is always the opportunity to make things better. Using the Happy Every Day Method helps you improve your score.

The Happy Every Day Method is a self-assessment technique for evaluating different aspects of your life. It serves to help you identify areas where you feel you need more fulfillment. It goes like this:

1. Evaluate one aspect of your life as if you are holding it in your hands.

2. Bring your attention to your body while taking deep, calm breaths, and notice any physical sensations or discomfort that may arise as you focus on this area of your life.

3. Assess your level of fulfillment in that area on a scale of 1-10, with one being the least fulfilled and ten being the most fulfilled.

4. Reflect on the reasons for your score and what changes need to be made to reach a 10/10 level of fulfillment in that area.

Repeat this process for all areas.

Next, bring these principles into your emotions by visualizing how a score of 10 in each area would feel. Your brain will naturally act to make that 10/10 score a reality. Increase the intensity of this activity. Visualize having the best day ever, where everything you want comes to fruition easily. When you imagine this scenario, pay attention to the feelings that arise in your body. Feel the sense of lightness, freedom, flow, and contentment. These feeling guideposts will help you stay focused on your goals.

The Happy Every Day method is another layer on your journey to bring together self-awareness (this is how I want to feel), self-acceptance (I have the right to feel this good), and self-confidence (I have the power to change what I need to feel this good.)

Taking conscious, deliberate action to decrease the deficiency in any area of your life is a great act of self-love. It's how you take care of yourself.

CHAPTER 10

Whatever Arises will Subside

This year I turned 60. I remember my father, when he turned 60, saying to me, "Am I really this old already? I still feel like I'm 30!"

I feel better than when I was 30 because now, I know who I am. Back then, I was just existing like a leaf being blown about. Unsure of myself, unable to speak my truth and call out bad behavior. I abused my body. I didn't eat correctly or rest when I should have. And my frame of mind was off as well. I was becoming familiar with my childhood trauma and not doing well at it. I didn't have the tools, and there was no therapist out there who was aware of the effects of childhood trauma yet.

So no, I don't wish to go back there. I am so grateful that I had to take this path to heal myself and then to be able to share this knowledge with you. We now have so many options that it may seem very confusing what to do. Take your time, absorb what you can, and let go of the rest for now.

All Parts of You are Welcome

Along your journey to self-love, you may go through dark periods. Know that this will pass. Your task is to maintain the courage to keep moving toward the light on the other side. During these times, you will face struggles, like pulling off layers of an onion, and there may be some tears. You may feel like you can't do it. Take a breath, and get grounded. Acknowledge how much work you've done already. One breath at a time. This is your journey.

The reward for your staying power is waiting for you at the other end of the obscurity. With each step toward the light, the darkness that once consumed you will further dissipate. You may be tired at this juncture, but you will also feel a sense of renewed energy, strength, and warmth that can only emanate from true love the closer you get.

The positive feelings will only intensify when you find your true self waiting for you beyond the dark. Embrace this being. You have returned home - to yourself. This feat is only possible when you realize that all along, love and compassion were right there in you. Whole now, you can continue on this journey of self-love, reaching for higher levels of consciousness and higher frequencies of energy.

Walk toward Higher Love

Life is a journey every single one of us walks. We pick up the pieces lost along the way to return to the most authentic version of ourselves. The journey is more satisfying when we walk together. Shared knowledge of how to get to the true self unites us. Trust that your new community will show up to support you.

Self-awareness is the first step we all take toward this common goal. Increase your self-awareness by exploring and understanding your ancestral story. Learning about your family history and cultural background gives you a deeper understanding of yourself and where you come from. This knowledge provides a sense of grounding and creates a connection between your past and present. With this foundation, you can better understand and accept yourself as you are now to develop yourself to be better for your future.

When we discover and accept our story, flaws, and all, we open ourselves to change and growth. To have a new story, you then have a new paradigm. Grounding yourself in this acceptance is necessary for your body and mind to calm down and be open to moving to the lighter, higher vibrations.

The next step on the journey to self-love is self-acceptance. This is the time when you clean up your house and remove any toxic influences that are holding you back - including people, negative thoughts, and unhealthy habits such as poor diet. Cleaning up your house elevates your energy and helps release any toxins you have accumulated because of those ties. Good energy feeds itself, and yours will expand to fill the space in your life.

Self-acceptance also means making choices that align with your values and goals and being comfortable with your appearance and perceived imperfections. You learn to let go of the fears that stop you from pursuing your passions and ambitions and make decisions that prioritize your well-being. By default, a positive and nurturing environment is created where you can flourish and grow.

Once you have achieved self-awareness and self-acceptance, you move on to the final step in the journey toward self-love: self-confidence. With self-awareness and self-acceptance, you clearly understand who you are, what you stand for, and what is important to you. This knowledge lets you speak your truth and assert yourself confidently and authentically. When you are self-confident, you set and refine your boundaries with yourself and with others. You say no when necessary and protect your time and energy. You stand your ground and look out for your best interests, and so, you trust yourself and your decisions, unswayed by the opinions of others.

With self-confidence, you will lift all areas of your life. You will become more successful in your career, have healthier relationships, and find purpose as you become surer in your ability to navigate challenges and setbacks. You will feel a sense of personal power and assuredness and walk through life with your head held high no matter what.

This person – the self-aware, self-accepting, and self-confident one – is the one who you get closer to with every step you take on your journey. With integrity and the persistent effort highlighted by the practices outlined throughout the chapters of this book, you can get to her sooner rather than later. Set aside any discouragement you feel while getting to her by reminding yourself that self-love is not a destination. The road never ends, so time, effort, patience, and gentleness are required.

We, women, are strong creatures no matter our race, background, age, or current circumstances. We are even stronger as a community providing guidance and support to each other. This book is a tool that aims to bring us closer together, united through the similar issues we face and the goals we want to achieve.

Remember, you are never alone on your journey. I, along with this book, am here to aid you. We are in this together. Reach out and share your story with me. Help another woman get closer to finding herself by recommending this book or leaving a review.

Thank you for joining me
on this journey to self-love.

—Diana xo

FINAL AWARENESS PRACTICE

Sitting with your back straight, feet on the ground, hands on your lap or left hand on your heart, right hand on your belly. Take 3 deep cleansing breaths.

Ask yourself these questions:

1. Who am I? What am I?

Am I the changing body

Or am I the awareness that experiences the changing body?

Am I the changing mind

Or am I the awareness in which the changing mind is the experience?

Am I my evolving personality

Or am I the awareness in which even my personality is a changing process?

Who am I? What am I?

What is it that wants to know the answer?

2. What do I want?

Be aware of the sensations or thoughts that arise and then let them go....

What do I want?

3. What is my purpose?

Why do I exist? Just be aware of any feeling or thought that may arise and let it go.

What is my purpose?

4.What am I grateful for?

Let this question open your heart.

Allow the feelings, thoughts or sensations to come and let them go.

Now repeat your name to yourself.

Remind yourself that this is my name and not who I am.

No form, just awareness.

Repeat – I AM

Repeat the vibration – OHM, OHM, OHM

Then let it go... what's left is awareness.

That's who you are....

Bring your awareness to your body and say:

Joyful energetic body

Put your hand on your heart and say:

Loving Compassionate heart

Bring your awareness to your third eye between your eyebrows and say:

Quiet reflective creative mind

Bring your awareness to your crown chakra at the top of your head and say:

Joyful lightness of being

REFERENCES

Beginning Note

1. *Age and Gender Differences in Self-Esteem* (n.d.). American Psychological Association(APA).(n.d.) https://www.apa.org/pubs/journals/releases/psp-pspp0000078.pdf

2. *White, rich men are the least depressed; poor women the most.* (2018, February 14). NBC News. https://www.nbcnews.com/health/health-news/women-twice-likely-men-have-depression-survey-finds-n847556

Chapter 1

3. *Teens, technology and romantic relationships.* (2020, May 30). Pew Research Center: Internet, Science & Tech. https://www.pewresearch.org/internet/2015/10/01/teens-technology-and-romantic-relationships/

4. Census.gov. (n.d.).https://www.census.gov/content/dam/Census/library/visualizations/time-series/demo/families-and-households/ms-2.pdf

5. *Divorce statistics and facts | What affects divorce rates in the U.S.?* (2022, March 3). Wilkinson & Finkbeiner, LLP. https://www.wf-lawyers.com/divorce-statistics-and-facts/

6. U.S. *Census* Bureau. (2021, April 22). *Marriage, divorce, widowhood remain prevalent among older populations.* Census.gov. https://www.census.gov/library/stories/2021/04/love-and-loss-among-older-adults.html#:~:text=With%20marriage%20comes%20the%20risk,about%2043%25%20for%20both%20sexes

7. Anodea Judith, *Eastern Body Western Mind: Psychology and the Chakra System as a Path to the Self* (New York: Celestial Arts, a division of Random House, 1996)

8. Martha Beck, *The Way of Integrity, Finding The Path To Your True Self* (New York: Penguin Life,2021)

Chapter 2

9. Discovery of "thought worms" open window to the mind.(July 13, 2020) https://www.queensu.ca/gazette/stories/discovery-thought-worms-opens-window-mind

10. *Adult Neuroplasticity: More than 40 years of research.* (n.d.). PubMed Central (PMC). https://www.ncbi.nlm.nih.gov/pmc/articles/PMC4026979/

11. Jan, M. (n.d.). *Secure attachment – from childhood to adult relationships.* Study Guides for Psychology Students - Simply Psychology. https://www.simplypsychology.org/secure-attachment.html

12. Yehuda and Lehrner, (Pubmed, 2018),*Intergenerational transmission of trauma effects: putative role of epigenetic mechanisms.* https://www.ncbi.nlm.nih.gov/pmc/articles/PMC6127768/

13. Thomas Hübl, *Healing collective trauma: a process for integrating our intergenerational and cultural wounds.*(Boulder, CO: Sounds True, 2020)

Chapter 3

14. Colin Tipping, *Radical Forgiveness* (Boulder, CO: Sounds True, 2009)

Chapter 4

15. Elle Magazine - Canada– March 16,2020, Empowered, Experienced & Full of Fire, page 82,

16. *Statistics research eating disorders.* (n.d.). https://www.nationaleatingdisorders.org/statistics-research-eating-disorders

17. *Eating disorder statistics.* (2022, June 8). National Association of Anorexia Nervosa and Associated Disorders. https://anad.org/eating-disorders-statistics/

18. *Preventing adverse childhood experiences.* (2021, August 23). Centers for *Disease* Control and Prevention. https://www.cdc.gov/vitalsigns/aces/index.html

19. *Stress, cortisol, and other appetite-related hormones: Prospective prediction of 6-month changes in food cravings and weight.* (n.d.). PubMed *Central* (PMC). https://www.ncbi.nlm.nih.gov/pmc/articles/PMC5373497/

20. Exercise for Mental Health. *PubMed* Central (PMC). Accessed January 17, 2023. https://www.ncbi.nlm.nih.gov/pmc/articles/PMC1470658/

21. *Bliss point (food).* (2023, January 3). Wikipedia, the free encyclopedia. Retrieved January 11, 2023, from https://en.wikipedia.org/wiki/Bliss_point_(food)

Chapter 5

22. A comprehensive definition for metabolic syndrome (April 2009). The Company of Biologists. https://journals.biologists.com/dmm/article/2/5-6/231/2213/A-comprehensive-definition-for-metabolic-syndrome

23. *Functional correlates of self-reported energy levels in the health, aging and body composition study.* (n.d.). PubMed Central (PMC). https://www.ncbi.nlm.nih.gov/pmc/articles/PMC8531104/

24. *Association between physical activity and risk of depression.* (2022, June 1). JAMA Network | *Home* of JAMA and the Specialty Journals of the American Medical Association. https://jamanetwork.com/journals/jamapsychiatry/fullarticle/2790780

25. The Human Garage. https://humangarage.net/

Chapter 6

26. Clinical Perspectives on Neurobiological Effects of Psychological Trauma. (Accessed Jan.2023). https://link.springer.com/article/10.1023/B:NERV.0000028082.13778.14

27. TED: Ideas Worth Spreading. Accessed January 13, 2023. https://www.ted.com/talks/amy_cuddy_your_body_language_may_shape_who_you_are/

Chapter 7

28."Hyperthyroidism, Hypothyroidism, and Cause-Specific Mortality in a Large Cohort of Women." PubMed Central (PMC). Accessed January 21, 2023. https://www.ncbi.nlm.nih.gov/pmc/articles/PMC5564026/

29. "Life Event, Stress and Illness." PubMed Central (PMC). Accessed January 13, 2023. https://www.ncbi.nlm.nih.gov/pmc/articles/PMC3341916/.

Chapter 8

30. Sexual harassment: Violence against women in the workplace. APA Psychnet. Accessed Jan.22, 2023. https://psycnet.apa.org/record/1994-11711-001?doi=1

31. *Social media use and anxiety in emerging adults*.Science Direct. Accessed Jan. 22,2023.

32. *Lisa* A. Phillips. "The Endless Breakup" (May7, 2019) Psychology Today. https://www.psychologytoday.com/us/articles/201905/the-endless-breakup

Chapter 9

33. Brendan Burchard, *High Performance Habits: How Extraordinary People Become That Way* (California:Hay House, Inc. 2017)

ABOUT THE AUTHOR

DIANA MIKAS is on a mission to change how we do love. For the better part of a decade, she has worked with women worldwide to regain their emotional and energetic equilibrium and find the love of their lives again. Her approach is holistic and multi-faceted as she brings in the wisdom of over 30 years of personal work, including her disciplines as a Usui Shiki Ryoho Reiki Master-level practitioner, Registered Holistic Nutritionist, and several years of Life Coaching practice.

Diana is the host of the Higher Love podcast found on Apple podcasts, Spotify or your favorite platform.

For more resources and to join the supportive Wholehearted community visit www.dianamikas.com.

Made in the USA
Monee, IL
12 July 2023